Bench Notes III

A Judge's Reflections for His Grandchildren on His Enduring Cases

Judge Paul A. Chernoff (Ret.)

I dedicate this book to four individuals who face special challenges in their lives:

David Chernoff, my son;
Dhillon Chernoff, my grandson;
Andrew Spector, my cousin;
and
Leo Ikoribitungaza, a burn victim from Burundi who calls me
"Grandpa Paul."

Bench Notes III: A Judge's Reflections for His Grandchildren on His Enduring Cases

Copyright © 2016 by Judge Paul A. Chernoff

ISBN: 978-1-4951-9524-2

Printed in the United States of America.

Cover design by Jonathan Cahill.

TABLE OF ENDURING CASES

PREFACE

The evil that men do lives after them;
the good is oft interred with their bones.[1]

Recently, I studied Shakespeare's three Roman plays: *Coriolanus,*
Antony and Cleopatra, and *Julius Caesar* on Sunday afternoons at
Brandeis University with Professor Michael Booth. Reading and
viewing Mark Anthony's funeral oration provided the inspiration and
theme for this third *Bench Notes* book. I came to realize that the
judicial errors that some attributed to me will live forever in the 125
published appellate decisions that can be found in legal texts and
digital archives. However, these written published decisions
comprise only a tiny fraction of the cases I handled. I refer to these
few as my Enduring Cases. The good that I did in the 10,000–15,000
other cases I touched in over nearly forty years of judging is long
forgotten and will be interred with my bones.

What follows is my memory of the more compelling cases that
are retrievable online or in law library texts. I have added a very few
others that may be memorable for the reasons the parties chose not to
appeal. This is not a personal accounting of myself. It is simply a
collection of stories; most are interesting, some are humorous, a few
are tragic, and many tend to show my fallibility.

An appellate court will affirm the trial judge if it finds no error
or where the error it finds is of little significance. The appellate court
will reverse and order a new trial where it finds that error might have
affected the verdict. Error was cited or criticism expressed in fewer
than one-half of my reported appellate cases. That might be about
average for trial judges. I caution the reader that one's appellate
batting average may be misleading. A courageous judge who is not
afraid to take on challenging matters will have more chances to err
than the more timid jurist who dodges the inside pitches.

---

[1] William Shakespeare, *Julius Caesar*, act iii, scene ii.

A Dog of a Witness

I have always loved dogs. Lynn and I ran the Boston Marathon with Betsy, our beloved standard poodle. I once had to judge the merits of a memorable Belgian Shepherd (Belgian Malinois) named Frisco, a certified narcotics dog that worked and lived with his K-9 police officer. Frisco was taught to respond to the scent of a narcotic drug by barking, scratching, and biting. He was given praise, pats, and treats when he "alerted" correctly. Frisco's sense of smell was extraordinary and he sometimes alerted to stale or trace odors. Since 40% of US paper currency contains traces of cocaine, a very sensitive narcotics dog might alert to perfectly innocent surroundings. Such a dog would require "extinction training."

The police had information from an informant that the defendant stored narcotic drugs at a public storage complex. Frisco was led past a row of 18 lockers and he "alerted" at the defendant's unit. Confident that the locker contained illicit drugs, the police sought a search warrant from a magistrate. To obtain the warrant, the police extolled the virtues of Frisco, citing his stellar training and performance. However, they neglected to reveal the negatives in his history.

With warrant in hand, the police searched the locker and found no evidence of narcotic drugs, but they did find a cache of illegal guns. The defendant was charged with possession of guns, which he sought to suppress as evidence on grounds that the search warrant was not legal. I found that the search was defective because important information was withheld from the magistrate. The government appealed, and the Appeals Court agreed with me.[2]

The legality of a search warrant depends upon the quality of the information given in writing to the judicial magistrate. A search is not made legal simply because it turns up the sought-after contraband, nor is it made illegal because it does not turn up what was sought. Had the magistrate been made aware of Frisco's total history, he might have required additional information before issuing the warrant. The magistrate was not made aware that Frisco most recently had "alerted" for both a baseball glove and a bag of papers that did not contain narcotics. The police overstated Frisco's reliability by incorrectly attributing 150 finds leading to the seizure of

---

[2] *Commonwealth v. Ramos*, 72 Mass. App. Ct. 773 (2009).

narcotics and the arrest of dealers. In fact, there were only 5 or 6 and the remaining "hits" occurred during training sessions. In addition, his handler had forewarned the other police officers at the storage complex to be careful because Frisco had a history of "false alerts." Moreover, the magistrate was not informed that Frisco lacked the "extinction" training that teaches dogs not to alert to stale smells.

My one regret is that I understand that Frisco was a congenial dog and I may have led to his early retirement.

A Belgian Malinois

Shh

The plaintiff widow was the sole caregiver for her adult paraplegic son who had been injured in an accident years earlier. She was no longer able to lift him and thus needed the daily assistance of a homecare worker costing $25,000 per year. Medicaid denied her application and instead indicated that it would pay the full price of a nursing home at $150,000 per year. She declined and appealed their decision. A state agency administers Medicaid within the state and a government attorney appeared in court to defend the agency's position. I could see that he did not have his heart in the case, but he was there to defend Medicaid's very broad discretion. After the court hearing, I felt that the widow should prevail and I informed my law clerk that we had to find a way to do the right thing.

After a day of research, the law clerk told me that the law was clearly against the widow and that I was compelled to rule in favor of the Department. When I said that I would not do so, she told me that ethically she could not work on a matter where the judge was bent on doing something illegal. I regret not explaining to her that it's not illegal to make a reasonable attempt at law reform to prevent an injustice. I called the administrative office and requested a different law clerk. My new clerk fully understood the challenge and together we crafted a decision that muted the dictates of the statute and relied on the legislative history and the preamble to the Medicaid law that states that one of its purposes was to keep families together.

To my new law clerk's dismay, I declined to send the decision for publication to the *Lawyers Weekly* newspaper or to the *Superior Court Reporter*. My law clerk was proud of our work and quite disappointed when I would not allow her to use it as a writing sample when applying for her next job. She reluctantly accepted my explanation that my decision might be vulnerable if appealed, that the Appeals Court or the Supreme Judicial Court could well find that I had committed judicial error. I told her that the Department's attorney appeared uncomfortable with the government's position and if there were no publicity, he would likely not appeal. If the case decision were made public, I was sure he would fear that others with less compelling situations would appeal Medicaid rulings citing my reasoning.

In retrospect, the law clerk got over being angry, the government did not appeal, the widow got her homecare worker, and I was spared an appellate reversal.

Judge Paul A. Chernoff

My Slippery Slope

Since the 1970s, I have engaged in the masochistic ritual of New England winter running. It starts as early as November. (I remember running through the streets of Boston during a snowy Thanksgiving Day road race.) It can persist to May, at least it did in 1977 when I ran in the wake of the Mother's Day blizzard. I have run, slid, slipped, and fallen on surfaces covered with snow, slush, and ice as I trod on roads, sidewalks, and unpaved paths. I'm annoyed with people who do not clear their sidewalks and force me either to run on their unsafe walks or on a busy roadway. Our justice system didn't help by exempting careless people from responsibility where an accident occurs on a "natural accumulation of ice or snow." I set out to do something about this two decades ago and got rebuffed by our highest court.

It stopped snowing in the town of Brookline by midnight. At the town's health center, the crew shoveled a layer of snow from the pedestrian ramp but left behind a layer of ice. This made the ramp more treacherous because they failed to cover the ice with sand. The plaintiff brought his daughter to the clinic around 8:30 AM. When leaving, he slipped and fell on ice near the bottom of the ramp and was injured. He sued and, in a trial before me, the jury found the town liable and awarded damages. The town asked me to overturn the verdict on grounds that it was not responsible for an injury occurring on a "natural accumulation of ice and snow." I denied their request. To me, they had disturbed the "natural accumulation" and it was tantamount to the town creating the icy walkway. The town appealed and the Appeals Court agreed with me. The town then appealed to our highest court. The Supreme Judicial Court reversed the Appeals Court, holding that I erred in not overturning the jury's verdict.[3]

It seemed unfair to me that the justice system was bending over backward to protect careless people who fail to keep their property safe. One appellate case excused a building owner where someone slipped on a driveway that was covered with ice that came from snowmelt from his roof. It was beyond me how that ice was seen as a natural accumulation.

Fortunately, the Supreme Judicial Court has recently removed the natural accumulation exemption. Nevertheless, we all should still tread carefully in winter.

---

[3] *Sullivan v. Town of Brookline,* 416 Mass. 825 (1994).

I'm a Person, Not a Thing

At three in the morning, the police observed a car proceeding slowly while weaving within its lane on Route 9 in Framingham. When the officer pulled alongside the vehicle, he saw that the passenger was leaning over the driver's lap with her head and shock of red hair bobbing up and down. The driver was cited for a violation known as Impeded Operation. According to Chapter 90, Section 13 of the statute,

> *No person, when operating a motor vehicle, shall permit to be on or in the vehicle or on or about his person anything which may interfere with or impede the proper operation of the vehicle.*

This provision was commonly used to cite a driver who carried cargo that blocked his view out the rear window or who hung large objects from the rearview mirror such as foam dice.

In court, the defendant driver was accompanied by his attractive red-headed girlfriend. The legal issue before me was whether she qualified as "anything" under the statute as the legislature could have been more precise and drafted a statute that prohibited "any person or any thing" from impeding operation of the vehicle. A defendant must receive the benefit of an ambiguity in a statute. I dismissed the case.

The prosecutor indicated that the government was going to appeal. However, after meeting with prosecutors from other counties, it was later decided not to appeal because an unfavorable ruling from the appellate court could jeopardize years of cases brought under that statute. Now, decades later, the wording of the statute remains the same.

Heavy on the Metal

As a district court judge, I was often assigned to motor vehicle traffic sessions. Of the hundreds of speeding cases I heard over the years, only one was appealed to a higher court. On August 19, 1976, a woman was issued a speeding citation after the police radar gun indicated that she was traveling 75 mph in a 55 mph zone. She contested the ticket and at her trial before me, her lawyer challenged the radar device that had an internal checking system that calibrated and reset the machine every hour. I admitted the results into evidence along with the officer's estimate of her speed and found her guilty and imposed a fine. The driver appealed.[4]

The Massachusetts Supreme Judicial Court upheld my decision, but agreed with the woman's lawyer that some kind of external checking procedure or external calibrating device was also necessary. The appellate court ruled that in the future, the police would have to show something more than an internal calibration. They affirmed my decision because there was no judicial guidance at that time as to radar. That case changed the requisites for radar evidence in court for decades to come.

---

[4] *Commonwealth v. Whynaught*, 377 Mass. 14 (1979).

Judged by My Peers

As a judge, I sometimes feel that I am the one being judged from all directions. From above, the appellate courts review transcripts of what I say, write, and do. Lawyers, citizens, and court staff observe me up close in the courtroom and formally evaluate me periodically. The media, which publically reports on me, always has its eyes and ears open. The Judicial Conduct Commission and the State Ethics Commission are also there to judge me if there is a complaint. I may also be assigned a colleague to observe me as part of a mentoring program. In addition to all of that, my sentencing is subject to formal review by an appellate body composed of my peers.

The Chief Justice of the Superior Court appoints three judges of the Superior Court to sit a few days each month as an appellate court to review sentences. An inmate can appeal to the Appellate Division of the Superior Court and complain that the judge imposed a sentence that was excessively harsh. The Appellate Division has the jurisdiction to lower or raise the sentence.[5] However, in the vast majority of sentencing appeals the Appellate Division does not change the sentence.

Judge James McDaniels served for many years on the Appellate Division. He used to tell me that, compared to others, I was a "light hitter" when it came to sentencing. Jim regaled me with the story of one hearing where the defendant was appealing my sentence. Jim said that he casually asked the lawyer and his client if they really thought that I had it in me to impose an excessive sentence. The inmate nodded "yes" and the three-judge panel laughed out loud. The lawyer whispered to his client and then withdrew the sentencing appeal. He must have thought they were about to increase the sentence.

Just like racehorses, judges have track records for almost everything, including sentencing practices, patience, competence, compassion, and work habits, as well as treatment of court staff, lawyers, and citizens. It all comes down to reputation and it doesn't hurt any of us to have a good one.

---

[5] In *Gavin v. Chernoff et al*, 546 F.2d 457 (1976), the federal appellate court ruled that the Appellate Division could increase a sentence without giving an explanation. I was a technical defendant in that case because Gavin was "confined" on parole and I was the head of the Parole Board.

Bewitched, Bothered, and Bewildered

The police had reliable information that the defendant was dealing drugs from a certain vehicle. They often observed this vehicle in front of the defendant's house and tried to follow him, but he used counter-surveillance techniques to evade them. However, one day the police were able to follow the man from his house and observed two drug transactions he made from his vehicle. They found the drugs on each of the buyers.

Somewhat later, when they arrested the defendant in his car while selling drugs to a third person, the police found drugs on the buyer and cash and drug paraphernalia with traces of a powdered drug in the vehicle. The defendant gave the name of John Doe and said he was homeless and that he would not disclose the vehicle's owner. He vociferously insisted that the officers take him to the police station so he could use a phone. From his conduct, the officers concluded that the man was intent on calling his home for the purpose of having someone there dispose of the drugs. The police immediately went to the man's house. There was no response to their knock so the police opened the door with the man's house key. They found his girlfriend and packages of drugs in plain view in the living room.

The defendant's attorney claimed that the police entered the defendant's home without sufficient information that there were drugs on the premises. I set out all of the information known to the police at the time of the entry and concluded that it was good police work that led to the discovery of the drugs. I denied the motion to suppress the drugs and the defendant was convicted and sentenced. He appealed.

The Appeals Court found that I had erred in my rulings and that the police had insufficient evidence to conclude there were drugs in the defendant's home.[6] The defendant's insistence on using a phone at the time of his arrest was an important factor to me in my written decision where I concluded that there was insufficient time to seek a search warrant. The appellate court wrote that I could not

---

[6] *Commonwealth v. Bookman,* 17 Mass. App. Ct. 546 (2010). At trial, the government introduced drug certificates from the state laboratory to prove the identity of the drug. The law permitting this was ruled unconstitutional by the US Supreme Court between the time of the trial and the appellate decision. So, the defendant in any event was entitled to a new trial. *Melendez-Diaz v. Massachusetts,* 557 US 305 (2009).

infer that the defendant was intent on calling his home and that perhaps he had wanted to call his lawyer or dispose of a stash of drugs kept somewhere other than at his home.

Some of my colleagues were bewitched, bothered, and bewildered that the Appeals Court had not credited the reasonable inferences drawn by experienced officers and by a judge who has dealt with these issues for decades. They asked me whether I was angry about the appellate decision and I told them most candidly that I was not angry, offended, or embarrassed.[7] It was part of a process that I signed on to and respected. I suppose it was like being called out on a close play at home plate and not arguing with the umpire.

---

[7] On the other hand, a decision questioning my judicial conduct would very much concern me. Thank heavens I was never complained against to the Judicial Conduct Commission.

Convicts in the Cloud

Some time ago, I read that a drug offender who had been found guilty at a trial before me died in prison while his case was on appeal and that the drug conviction had been vacated and the appeal dismissed by the Appeals Court. I remember musing that perhaps they let him meet his maker without the stigma of the criminal conviction. I also thought we would never find out whether I committed judicial error at trial.

It is odd that the law seems to forgive convicted persons who die during the pendency of their appeals and that the law has not changed in recognition of society's increased sensitivity to victims' rights.

More than twenty years ago, a deranged murderer killed two persons and wounded five others when firing a rifle at workers at two Planned Parenthood clinics. The convicted murderer later committed suicide in prison while his murder convictions were pending appeal. In another case, a defrocked priest, convicted of molesting several children, was murdered in prison while his cases were pending appeal. Their appellate cases were deemed moot and dismissed, and their respective convictions for murder and child rape were vacated and dismissed. There was a hue and cry from victims, their families, and advocacy groups to change the law through legislation. Despite a promise of legislative action, no change resulted. The appeal stemming from the "Marathon Bomber's" murder convictions will likely take several years. Whether Dzhokar Tsarnaev will live to the date of his court-ordered execution is problematical considering that the appellate process for murder cases is lengthy and his life could be cut short by unnatural causes such as suicide or murder. There would be a national public reaction to the vacating of his convictions.[8]

This centuries old practice is rooted in the English Common Law and is known as the "Abatement Doctrine." It is the law in Massachusetts and in many states and federal districts, but not in my native Connecticut. I used to think that it was part of a benevolent forgiveness by government. Now, I realize that it is merely a judicial tradeoff for not having to resolve pending appellate cases rendered less important by the death of a litigant. For some, it may be seen as a

---

[8] The outspoken families of convicted organized crime boss Whitey Bulger's victims would certainly be heard should his convictions be vacated because his death preceded resolution of his appeals.

lose-lose situation in that the convicted person's family loses the opportunity to seek vindication and the victim loses the satisfaction of the conviction and the opportunity to use it in a civil action against the defendant's estate. There is no theological underpinning for a practice that forgives only those who die during their legal appeal. The only clear winner is the court system in that it is relieved of a time-consuming appeal.

Hearing the Boston Symphony Orchestra

The Boston Symphony Orchestra (BSO), one of the most revered institutions in all of Boston, was in serious legal difficulty. It was about to be sued by actress Vanessa Redgrave, whose contract to narrate performances of Stravinsky's *Oedipus Rex* was canceled by the BSO. The BSO's actions were in response to community pressure concerning Redgrave's public statements supporting the Palestine Liberation Organization to the detriment of Israel.

The BSO looked to its insurer to provide a legal defense to the anticipated lawsuit. The insurance company engaged the services of an independent law firm to advise it whether, under the policy, it was obligated to defend the BSO. The firm's legal advice was that the company was not obliged to defend the BSO. The insurance company denied coverage and the BSO sued the company, demanding that it defend them and that they pay the BSO multiple damages under the Consumer Protection Act for wrongfully denying coverage.

The insurance company moved before me to dismiss both the action to require them to defend the BSO and the Consumer Protection Action. After much research, I disagreed with the advice given to the insurance company by the law firm and I directed them to defend the BSO on the Redgrave suit that had been filed. I did agree with the company that it should not be liable for damages under the Consumer Protection Act even though they refused to defend the BSO when, to my mind, the policy obligated them to do so. To me, the fact that they sought legal assistance from an independent law firm protected them from a consumer claim.

The company felt that I had erred in ruling that they were obliged to defend the BSO and appealed. The BSO also appealed, submitting that I committed an error in denying them the right to prove a consumer protection violation at a trial. The case was closely watched by the legal community, which has an interest in how insurance policies are construed and whether a judge could rule on the merits of a Consumer Protection Act matter without a trial. The Supreme Judicial Court affirmed both of my rulings and required the insurance company to defend the BSO and they let stand my order dismissing the consumer protection claim.[9]

---

[9] *Boston Symphony Orchestra, Inc. v. Commercial Union Insurance Co.*, 406 Mass. 7 (1989).

To this day, I feel very privileged to have served as a trial judge with the opportunity and responsibility of ruling in precedent-setting cases.

Boston Symphony Hall

The Peter Principle

A lawyer in the Attorney General's office told me recently that I am routinely quoted in courtrooms, not for my decision in a celebrated murder case nor for a landmark employment discrimination case, but for an obscure sex case.

The penile plethysmograph is an electronic device that wraps around one's penis and accurately measures changes in its size and tumescence that are directly related to male sexual arousal. The subject of the test is usually a person who has committed a sex crime and the purpose of the test is to determine whether his sexual offender therapy has been successful and whether he is currently dangerous.

With the device in place, the subject sits in a chair and views videos of "normal" stimuli such as explicit adult sex. He also views "deviant" stimuli such as depictions of scantily clad children and "neutral" stimuli such as landscape scenery.

In the case before me, therapists were prepared to give opinions as to whether the defendant was currently sexually dangerous. A sex therapist retained by the defendant concluded that sexual offender treatment had been successful because the defendant was no longer aroused by "deviant" stimuli and his arousal by "normal" stimuli was also an indicator that he was cured. A government therapist was prepared to testify that the results of another plethysmograph test showed some arousal with "deviant" stimuli. I excluded reference to plethysmograph testing by both therapists.

I wrote a decision declaring that neither a defense nor a government expert could rely on the result of a plethysmograph test in court because there is no credible scientific data that indicates that a person who is aroused by "deviant" stimuli has a proclivity towards sexual misconduct.[10] Also, there is no evidence that a person who shows arousal with "normal" rather than "deviant" stimuli is "cured" and is less likely to commit a sexual crime against children.

---

[10] *Commonwealth v. Damiano*, 40 Mass. App. Ct. 801 (1996). The appellate case affirms the conviction and the validity of the defendant's guilty plea that led to the prison term he was serving during my release hearing. My decision is noteworthy because each side, for their own reasons, decided to not appeal. They saved the issue for another day and another case that never came.

Although my written decision was never appealed, it has served as precedent as if it were an appellate decision. For decades, other judges have been routinely excluding plethysmograph evidence in court cases. It's nice to be seen as an authority on something. I just wish it were something else.

A Million Bucks

Cancer claimed the life of the middle-aged man on Bastille Day, July 14. When the man's widow sought the tax-free proceeds from his one-million-dollar life insurance policy, the insurance company refused to pay, claiming the policy was invalid.

In the spring of the previous year, the husband filed an application through an insurance agent for one million dollars of life insurance with his wife as beneficiary. The insurance agent waited until July 17 to file the application for insurance with a Canadian company that did not require a physician's examination. The company approved the policy on August 4. Five days later, on August 9, the man learned he had colon cancer. He did not disclose this diagnosis to the insurance company and the policy was delivered to the man on August 30. He died almost one year later.

It was for me to decide whether the widow should receive at least one million dollars or nothing at all. The insurance company relied on the language of the insurance contract while the widow's attorney relied on the language of the state statute.

The insurance policy stated that there would be no payment unless the statements in the application were still true at the time the policy issued. According to the insurance company, the man's failure to inform them of his changed health status while the application was pending invalidated the policy.

The state statute provided that where an insurer does not require a previous medical examination, statements made in the application as to the physical condition of the applicant shall be held valid absent a finding of fraud. Here, both parties stipulated that there was no fraud.

I ruled in favor of the widow, finding that the language of the contract had to yield to the state statute, especially because the contract language was overly broad. I posited that if the husband had died of cancer thirty years rather than one year later, the policy language would still justify denying coverage decades later. I also denied the widow's claim that the insurance company, in refusing to pay on the policy, violated the consumer protection law that would have entitled her to double or treble damages plus attorney's fees. Hence, my judgment awarded the widow one million dollars plus interest.

The insurance company lawyer felt I had erred by not invalidating the policy and giving the widow nothing. The widow's attorney felt I had erred by not finding a violation of the consumer protection statute and awarding two or three million dollars. I felt it was a close case and that the Appeals Court might affirm my decision or reverse it in favor of the plaintiff widow or in favor of the defendant insurer. Each attorney appealed and after one year I was perplexed that there was no appellate decision. I later learned that the attorneys settled the case for an unpublished amount and withdrew their respective appeals.

Violating Probation Before It Starts

It's not uncommon to sentence a person to incarceration on one offense and a term of probation on a second offense effective after the first sentence is served. For example, a person could be sentenced to one year for breaking into someone's car and placed on probation for two years for stealing the car radio. The two-year probationary period is consecutive and starts when the person is released after serving the one-year sentence. If he violates the terms and conditions of his probation, then he can be sentenced to prison on the car radio case.

I sentenced a defendant in that manner. While serving his prison sentence, he committed a very serious crime. He tried to hire someone to kill his wife. He arranged this through a fellow prisoner who instead reported him to the police. A state police trooper posed as the "hit man" and visited the defendant in prison to seal the deal.

The probation officer and the prosecutor asked me to revoke the defendant's probation. The defendant's lawyer argued that his probation could not be revoked because he wasn't on probation when he committed his misdeed in prison. I could find no legal precedent on whether a person could be sentenced for violating terms of probation that hadn't started yet. I revoked the man's probation and imposed a sentence reasoning that he was implicitly on unsupervised probation while serving his sentence.

The Supreme Judicial Court agreed.[11] Since then, out of an abundance of caution, many judges start the probationary term running when the person enters prison. That term is said to run concurrently with the committed sentence. I thought that the appellate court might find that I had erred, but they didn't.

---

[11] *Commonwealth v. Phillips,* 40 Mass. App. Ct. 801 (1996).

All's Well That Ends Well

The defendant was a state senator and a long-time legislator who suddenly suffered a mental breakdown and, on a single day, he engaged in a bizarre series of events: he followed four women while uttering vulgar things to them and reached toward one woman's private area. He actually touched no one. The government charged the man with several misdemeanors and the felony of attempted indecent assault and battery, which was not a crime articulated in the criminal code. I suggested the omission in the code required that the defendant could only be charged with the misdemeanor of simple assault and I was proven to be wrong by the Supreme Judicial Court.

I certified a question to the Appeals Court asking if the prosecution could charge the man with the felony. Conviction of a felony would bar him from receiving retirement benefits even though he had paid money into the retirement system for over twenty years. The Supreme Judicial Court felt the issue was important enough to remove the case from the Appeals Court. The Supreme Judicial Court ruled that a catchall provision in another statute was sufficient to include attempted indecent assault and battery and hence it was an offense with which the man could be charged.[12] Their analysis was disappointing to me and in the instant case set up the defendant to lose his retirement income, which would be both a real hardship and an injustice.

This put the burden on me to find a just solution. On the one hand, the defendant had sought and was receiving treatment at a leading mental health facility. On the other hand, the case had attracted a great deal of public attention and there were interests that wanted to destroy him. The media mistakenly reported that the man had committed rape and other sexual assaults involving touching people that had not happened. Over the objection of the prosecution, I resolved the case in a manner that did not give the man a felony conviction. Instead, he received misdemeanor convictions, a short prison sentence, and a long period of probation supervision with specific conditions to ensure that the conduct would not be repeated.

---

[12] *Commonwealth v. Marzilli,* 457 Mass. 64 (2010).

No Good Deed Goes Unpunished

When sober, the man wasn't a bad sort, but alcohol turned him into a mean drunk who robbed and assaulted others. I was Chairman of the Parole Board and the other members were very reluctant to parole Raymond St. Onge because he had a long record and had failed before on parole. I convinced the members of the Parole Board that he might succeed this time. After all, he had completed an alcohol treatment program while in prison and he had been accepted to a therapeutic halfway house in the community.

We paroled St. Onge and, within a week, he reoffended. He was taken to the city jail and his parole officer initiated parole revocation proceedings. The parole staff failed to schedule an initial hearing at the jail and he was transported to the state prison system where he received a final revocation hearing. A panel of the Parole Board decided to revoke his parole and reinstate his prison sentence. I had no knowledge at the time that St. Onge had been arrested, sent to jail, or sent back to prison.

About one year later, I was appointed a judge of the Newton District Court. One evening, I received a call from an attorney from the Attorney General's office informing me that St. Onge had sued me for denying him a hearing at the jail. I was stunned to learn I had lost the lawsuit because his office, which represents state officials, had failed to respond to the lawsuit. The federal court had issued a judgment ordering me to pay St. Onge $25,000.[13] I told the lawyer that I wanted to appeal the judgment, even though there would be substantial interest accrued if I lost the appeal. Two months later I read in *Lawyers Weekly* that I lost my appeal because the Attorney General's office had failed to file a brief on my behalf. Now the judgment against me exceeded $30,000.

I complained to the chief lawyer at the Attorney General's office. He apologetically indicated that I could retain the services of a lawyer at government expense. I chose Steve Rosenfeld, a very highly regarded lawyer. It did not take him long to convince the federal judge and St. Onge's lawyer to reopen the case, remove me from the lawsuit, and settle the case with the Parole Board where the state would pay some amount of money.

---

[13] *St. Onge v. Chairman, Massachusetts Parole Board*, 634 F.2d 615 (1st Cir. 1980).

In retrospect, I made two errors: convincing others to parole a true recidivist and not having a back-up system to ensure timely parole revocation hearings in all cases.

Clairvoyance

For many years chemists rarely appeared in court on drug cases because their laboratory reports were admissible without their testimony. That changed abruptly in 2009 when the US Supreme Court ruled that the Massachusetts law and practice were unconstitutional because it deprived an accused person of the right of confrontation, that is, the right to face witnesses against him.

Eight years earlier in 2001, I had presided over a celebrated murder case where a doctor was convicted of murdering his wife. The DNA laboratory chemist in my case was in the courthouse but was not called to testify by either lawyer. Her certified test results were admitted into evidence and one of the foremost DNA experts then testified about the significance of the test results. The jury found the defendant guilty of first-degree murder and the Supreme Judicial Court affirmed the conviction in 2013.[14] In 2014, in a Michigan case, the US Supreme Court ruled that the right to confrontation applied to DNA testing too. This raised the question as to whether the new rule should be applied retroactively and upset many past cases including this one decided thirteen years earlier. When I tried to explain this to a non-lawyer friend, he thought it ridiculous that trial judges were supposed to be clairvoyant and anticipate that the law would change a dozen years later.

I certainly understand this. It's hard enough to figure out and apply the current law in the midst of the hustle and bustle of a trial. Nevertheless, there are times when a judge should suspect that some aspect of the current law may be in flux or is ripe for change. In my case the new law was not applied retroactively. Whew!

---

[14] *Commonwealth v. Greineder*, 464 Mass. 580 (2013).

Extreme Atrocity or Cruelty

At the time, I thought I had made an unpopular, courageous, difficult, and correct decision. The Supreme Judicial Court subsequently ruled I was wrong and, in retrospect, I agree.[15]

The defendant, a low-functioning adult, brought his girlfriend and her 3-month-old baby girl to a New Year's Eve party at his mother's home. The defendant was intoxicated when he was in the bedroom with the crying baby. He slammed the baby's head against a solid object, probably a dresser. With one or more blows, he caused a fracture of the baby's skull, loss of consciousness, and her subsequent death. The defendant was charged with first-degree murder. The jury rejected the government's theory of premeditated murder, but instead found the defendant guilty of murder by extreme atrocity or cruelty. Clearly, what he did was atrocious, but without premeditation a finding of first-degree murder rather than second-degree murder requires proof of extreme atrocity or cruelty. The law requires that the judge present seven factors to the jury. A finding of the presence of at least one factor is required to return a verdict of guilty to first-degree murder by extreme atrocity or cruelty.[16]

After the jury convicted the defendant of first-degree murder, I heard post-trial motions by the defense seeking: a finding of not guilty, an order for a new trial, or a finding of guilty to the lesser offense of second-degree murder or manslaughter. Both the prosecutor and the defense attorney were persuasive.

I rejected all defense requests except that of reducing the verdict to second-degree murder and I imposed a life sentence with the possibility of parole after fifteen years. I examined the evidence in light of the seven required factors and found that there was no basis in the evidence for five of the seven factors with only a theoretical basis for numbers 3 and 5. Both the government and the defendant appealed to the Supreme Judicial Court, which affirmed me on all of

---

[15] *Commonwealth v. Auclair*, 444 Mass. 306 (2005).
[16] The seven extreme atrocity or cruelty factors for the jury to consider are:
1. Indifference to and taking pleasure in the victim's suffering;
2. The victim's consciousness and degree of suffering;
3. Extent of injury;
4. Number of blows;
5. Manner and degree of force with which the blows were delivered;
6. The nature of the weapon, instrument, or method used; and
7. Disproportion between means needed to cause death and those employed.

my post-trial rulings except the reduction of the verdict. The appellate court found a basis for numbers 1, 3, and 4 and, in retrospect, I agree.

I have often wondered why, at the time, it wasn't clear to me that the issue was whether the evidence could persuade the jury of the existence of these factors. Whether it persuaded me or not was of no relevance.

When Only One Is a Pattern

It used to be that during jury selection each lawyer would exercise a certain number of preemptory challenges and excuse jurors without the permission of the judge and without offering any explanation or justification. Appellate courts changed this practice and now lawyers are precluded from excluding jurors because they belong to a constitutionally protected class that includes gender, race, religion, national origin, and ethnicity. It does not include classes based on age, so lawyers can still seek a younger or older jury. Sooner or later sexual preference will join the list of protected classes. Under the new procedure, lawyers must explain their reasons for challenging jurors in a protected class when there appears to be a pattern of challenging people in that class; for example, when a lawyer challenges four women and no men, the lawyer has the burden of showing the challenges were based on reasons other than gender.

In a murder case over which I presided, there was only one African-American in the entire jury pool. The prosecutor challenged a number of jurors including the black juror. It was not a particularly race-sensitive case as both the defendant and the victim were black. Since the prosecutor challenged only one minority juror, there was no pattern established of excluding persons in a protected class. I ruled that one was not a pattern so he did not violate the rule to the extent that I should disallow the challenge.

The defendant was convicted of second-degree murder and the Appeals Court found my jury selection process appropriate. The Supreme Judicial Court reversed the Appeals Court, holding that I had erred and that a pattern was not necessary to show a discriminatory process. I thought I was responsible for a new mathematics, that one can be a pattern.[17] A second trial was scheduled before me. However, the prosecution and defense avoided trial with a plea bargain where the defendant pled guilty to the lesser charge of manslaughter and received a substantially reduced sentence.

Over the years, there were two or three times when I was patted on the back by the Appeals Court with an affirmance and then, on further appeal, spanked by the Supreme Judicial Court with a reversal.

---

[17] *Commonwealth v. Stacey Harris,* 28 Mass. App. Ct. 764 (1990) Appeals Court, *Commonwealth v. Stacey Harris*, 409 Mass. 462 (1991) Supreme Judicial Court.

Guessed Wrong

In *Lipshitz v. Raytheon Corporation*, a female doctor at an industrial plant sued the company on grounds that a less qualified male physician was promoted instead of her to a supervisory position. That male physician allegedly spent company time reading novels and told his nurse he would examine only one eye and one ear during physical examinations to save time because, in his experience, when one eye or ear was normal, the other one was fine too.

When I tried the *Raytheon* case, Massachusetts was a "pretext" state in that the law allowed an employer to be found liable for employment discrimination merely because a terminated employee was not given the real reason for the termination or, in my case, the adverse action. Most of us knew it was unfair to sue an employer who simply chose not to embarrass the employee by disclosing the real reason for being fired, for example, when the employee had terrible body odor. We knew that the Supreme Judicial Court was looking for an opportunity to fashion a more appropriate standard and that the case might have to be tried twice.

I thought I could outsmart everyone. I would instruct the jury under the current law and then give them advisory questions to answer under the law that the Supreme Judicial Court would most likely fashion, that being the "pretext-plus" rule that was then the rule in the federal court. The lawyers did not think my plan to avoid two trials was so brilliant. Well, I did. I instructed the jury with "pretext" instructions and then instructed them with "pretext-plus" instructions as an advisory verdict.

I wasn't so smart after all. The jury found for the plaintiff under the "pretext" instructions. As to a verdict under the "pretext-plus" instructions, there was a hung jury as at least 12 of the 14 jurors could not agree on a result. The Supreme Judicial Court did indeed reverse the case and instituted a new procedure.[18] The court was kind to me in its decision, making it clear that my "pretext" instructions correctly followed the law they were now changing. It turned out the new rule adopted by the Supreme Judicial Court was not the federal "pretext-plus" rule. So, I guessed wrong.

---

[18] *Lipshitz v. Ratheon Corporation*, 434 Mass. 493 (2001).

Bottoms Up

Absent exigent or emergency circumstances, the police are only authorized to conduct a strip search of an arrested person in private environs.

The police had sufficient reason to arrest the defendant for drugs. It appeared that there was a "lump" in the back of the defendant's pants and that he was hiding something between his legs. The police at first tried to search him in a fairly private area, but the defendant eluded them. They finally tackled him on a sidewalk within full view of the general public. While the defendant was lying flat on his stomach, the police pulled his pants down, exposing his buttocks, and they recovered a packet of drugs from between his buttocks.

I ruled that exposing the buttocks of a person who was lying down on a public sidewalk constituted an invalid "strip search," which required that the evidence be suppressed. There was no indication that the man was armed or that he could destroy evidence. He should have been taken to a private place such as a room at the police station and searched there. The government disagreed and appealed. My decision was affirmed and the drugs were suppressed.[19]

This was a close case because the police should have some leeway in searching a person who is legally under arrest and appears to be secreting narcotics. It is an important case because it dealt with the competing interests of privacy and security in a public confrontation between a citizen and the police where there is a potential for the use of force and personal injury that can lead to tragic consequences. It is expected that the court's decisions in this area should guide law enforcement personnel.

---

[19] *Commonwealth v. Morales,* 462 Mass. 334 (2012).

Liar, Liar Pants on Fire

For years, Massachusetts was one of the very few states that gave limited approval to the use of the results of polygraph tests at trials. A criminal defendant who passed a lie detector test could have the results admitted at trial. Otherwise, lie detector results were inadmissible.

I was assigned the task of presiding over a hearing on three consolidated cases where the issue was the future use of the polygraph. The country's leading experts on the polygraph were called to testify. I initially had little confidence in polygraph devices and polygraph examiners. The government's position was that the polygraph was insufficiently reliable for court, even though government agencies were, and still are, using the polygraph internally in hiring employees and conducting internal investigations. After several days of testimony, I became impressed with the emerging science of lie detection and ruled that the current practice of limited approval should continue, but with a few caveats. The Supreme Judicial Court disagreed and barred polygraph evidence entirely.[20]

I don't think the appellate court really discounted the reliability of polygraph tests. After all, they are increasingly used in police investigations, employment applications, screening for sensitive positions, and for monitoring parolees. I think the court wanted to avoid the dynamic in the courtroom where machine results might be given inordinate weight by a lay jury. The theory of jury decision making is that the collective wisdom of the jury together with their collective centuries of human experience can and will determine the truth.

---

[20] *Commonwealth v. Mendes,* 406 Mass. 201 (1985).

When a Kid Is a Kid

A laid-off worker is entitled to collect unemployment compensation for a specified period or until the worker returns to the workforce. The worker is entitled to a supplemental dependency allowance for his or her spouse and each natural child or adopted child.

      I presided over a case where the laid-off worker was married to a widow with four children. Although he had not adopted his wife's children, the man had been their sole source of support and they qualified as his dependents at tax time. For many months, the Department of Employment Security included the dependent stepchildren when calculating the man's benefits. After he returned to the workforce, the Department notified the worker that he must return the amount he received for the dependent stepchildren because the law did not allow benefits for unadopted stepchildren. This amounted to hundreds of dollars that he could ill-afford to return. He appealed to the trial court and I was assigned the case.

      I felt there was an injustice attributable to an unfair law. Some of my more experienced colleagues advised me that judges must strive to uphold laws and leave it to the legislature to rectify bad ones. I could not abide by this and decided to protect these poor children by striking down the evil law with the cudgel of the United States Constitution. I wrote, to the bemusement of my colleagues, that the children were denied the equal protection of law guaranteed by the Bill of Rights as no data supported a proposition that unadopted stepchildren eat less than other children or that they do not require the same amount of clothing to protect them from harsh New England winters. My ruling directed the Department to allow the worker to keep the dependent stipend. The government appealed my decision to the Supreme Judicial Court which, to the amazement of some of my colleagues, affirmed my ruling.[21]

      The appellate court did not rule on my theory of the unconstitutionality of the state statute, but it did agree with me that the statute should be construed in a manner that promotes the purpose of the law, that is, treating stepchildren like other children. In other words, my roar turned into a meow, but a good one.

---

[21] *Roush v. Director of the Division of Employment Security and Others*, 377 Mass. 572 (1979).

A Good Deed Goes Punished

The defendant did not have much going for him when he was brought from jail to court for sentencing. There was little that could be said to mitigate punishment for his most recent housebreak. Minutes before I was to pass sentence, the attorneys asked if I would be willing to meet privately with them and two others in my office and I agreed. The two others turned out to be a police detective and a high-ranking correctional officer from the jail. I learned that the defendant had recently risked his life to thwart a plan by two extremely dangerous inmates to kidnap and harm a guard at the jail. I, of course, agreed to keep this information to myself as disclosure would put the defendant at very serious risk. The prosecutor indicated that he was still going to ask for a harsh sentence, but he would do so "quietly" and neither openly advocate for it nor comment if I imposed a lesser sentence.

I felt that the defendant deserved substantial consideration for his good deed, which may have saved a life at the expense of endangering his own. I constructed a rather unconventional sentence ensuring he would not have contact with inmates from the jail. The sentence was also substantially lower than that recommended by the prosecutor.

The next day all hell broke loose. Someone complained to the newspapers about the length of the sentence and a well-known, highly read columnist wrote a lengthy column in the statewide newspaper condemning me and suggesting that I deserved to have my own house broken into. According to the editorial, the columnist had contacted the prosecutor, who complained that my sentence was both inappropriately permissive and illegal and that he was going to file an appeal to the Supreme Judicial Court, and he did.

A judge is represented by the Attorney General's office when a prosecutor appeals a judge's decision. The attorney who was assigned to represent me called and said that she agreed with the prosecutor that my sentence was an illegal one and she was seeking my permission to "confess error" at the hearing, in other words, to admit that I was wrong and give in. I told her in no uncertain terms that I would not do so. As a former chairman of the Parole Board I knew the difference between a legal and an illegal sentence. I armed her with a sentencing memorandum to bring to the hearing before a single justice of the Supreme Judicial Court.

The afternoon after the hearing I received a call from the lawyer informing me that I had been affirmed. She said that she did not utter one word, that the judge listened to the prosecutor and simply said "denied," after which he shut off the table light and got up and left the bench. She asked if I had a special relationship with the judge. I replied that I hardly knew him but that obviously he could read between the lines and understand that there was an undisclosed something that supported the legality and rationality of the sentence.

The rest of the story is not so pleasant. Given the number of people who called to commiserate, I knew that my reputation had been sullied by the columnist. I could not trust the prosecutor who had gone back on his word. The defense lawyer had the gall weeks later to file a motion seeking a sentence reduction on grounds that I was too harsh. My clerk ran into the columnist weeks later and told him that he had really whacked someone who didn't deserve it. The columnist nodded and said he had since learned that the judge was "not a bad guy." What a sad commentary on editorial writing.

What Degree of Murder Is to Your Liking?

There are two kinds of murder: first-degree murder, which mandates a sentence of "natural life" (that is, the duration of one's life) in prison without parole, and second-degree murder, which also mandates life in prison but with a parole eligibility after service of fifteen years. Although each type of murder carries its own technical elements, our statute reads that, "the degree of murder shall be found by the jury." This means that the jury may return a verdict for second-degree murder even if the person technically committed first-degree murder.

In the case where I presided, the defendant was tried for the murder of a young high school student, the son of his girlfriend. The defendant was about 55 years old at the time and when the evidence was in and the case was to be decided by the jury, the defendant's attorney announced that the defendant wanted the jury to have only two choices for a verdict; that is, guilty of first-degree murder or not guilty. He feared the jury would likely render a compromise verdict of second-degree murder that would not give the defendant the possibility of parole release until he was over 70 years old. The prosecutor did not object to this choice and I so instructed the jury. Their deliberation was lengthy and people in the courthouse thought the defendant had made a wise choice and that he would be acquitted. Well, it turned out that the jury finally did convict him of first-degree murder.

On appeal, the Supreme Judicial Court ruled that the jury always, regardless of the evidence, has the option of returning a verdict of guilty to second-degree murder.[22] It affirmed the conviction, stating that from then on it would be reversible error for a judge not to give the jury the option of second-degree murder.

I received a similar "don't do it again" advisory from the Supreme Judicial Court twenty years earlier when I admitted evidence from a radar gun device in a speeding case (see page 7).

---

[22] *Commonwealth v. Vinnie*, 428 Mass. 161 (1998).

Where Is Abbey Road?

Richard returned from Vietnam disabled from exposure to Agent Orange and found himself immersed in another war, this one with his abutting neighbor, the Cistercian Abbey of the Strict Observance. At stake was ownership of a four-acre parcel of land between his mother's property and the seventy acres of the Abbey. Richard spent his days sitting by a campfire on the disputed property near the Abbey's driveway. His disheveled appearance and his worn camper were an eyesore to the fifty-five nuns and Abbey visitors. Richard spent his boyhood doing volunteer farm chores for the Abbey. Now, he and his mother were defending a civil suit by the Abbey that sought to evict him for trespassing.[23]

The trial before me without a jury was highly technical and complex. Even with the aid of a senior title examiner from the Land Court, I was unable to determine ownership of the portion of the parcel containing his camp. I learned that the deeds in that rural part of Norfolk County date from the 1820s and inadequately describe the size, configuration, and location of the land. Also, many of the deeds contain errors, especially as to the linear measurement of boundary lines. When the length of property lines is incorrect, one must rely on the description of monuments in the deed such as a stone wall, a large rock, a stream, or a barbed wire fence. Walking the area with my Land Court colleague, we found that many of the monuments described in the 1820 deeds no longer exist. We were unable to start at one corner and follow the deeds back to the starting place in order to establish the perimeter of the disputed property. Neither party convinced me that it owned the property to the exclusion of the other. Also, neither party proved ownership by adverse possession, occupying it for more than 20 years. Richard accused the Abbey of mounting a conspiracy against him by employing a biased surveyor. The Mother Superior responded that they loved Richard and prayed for him every day.

My twenty-page decision awarded the Abbey a 1.61-acre portion and found that there was insufficient evidence to establish ownership over the remaining 2.39 acres that contained the camp. Hence, neither party could exclude the other. I wrote that further relief might be available at the Land Court. Both parties felt that I had erred and instead chose a direct appeal of my decision. Months later a

---

[23] *Cistercian Abbey of the Strict Observance v. Burnett*, Norfolk Superior Court, Civil No. 05-2361 (July 2, 1998). Massachusetts Land Court, 21 LCR 352 (2013).

staff attorney at the Appeals Court commented to me that the case looked impossible. The staff attorney was relieved when the Appeals Court dismissed the appeal on the technical grounds of untimely filed briefs. Nine years later the parties sought review at the Land Court under a little used and outdated statute. After another six years, the Land Court ruled recently that Richard did not have ownership rights to the 2.39 acres of disputed land. That decision may well be pending appeal.

Well, Richard, at least you got an additional fifteen years on the property.

Given Credit Where It's Not Due

Most judges feel that they are too often blamed or criticized unfairly and that praise is uncommon. On a very rare occasion, a judge is given credit in the legal community and elsewhere when it is not due to him or her. That happened to me twice in nearly forty years.

The progress in the science of DNA testing had outstripped the legal system. I remember when the courts first recognized that DNA testing for determining paternity was far more exacting and accurate than the ABO blood testing that had been the standard test and could only exclude a putative father. As to the criminal law, it was agreed that the Supreme Judicial Court ought to consider the issue of the admissibility of DNA evidence in a test case where both the community of prosecutors and defense attorneys would have an opportunity for input. A motion to suppress the results of DNA testing was filed in Norfolk County and an experienced and very highly regarded judge was assigned to hear the motion. With the best and the brightest attorneys on each side of the issue, the judge conducted an evidentiary hearing where she heard from several expert witnesses on the reliability of the developing DNA science. The judge ruled that the evidence of the DNA match between the defendant's DNA and that found at the scene would be admissible at trial.

It turned out that by happenstance, I was assigned to the court session when the case was on for trial. With the DNA results admitted, the case was an open and shut one on the issue of guilt. The defendant waived a jury trial on the advice of his attorney and his nonjury trial proceeded before me. It was a foregone conclusion that the evidence was so strong against the defendant that his trial was merely a vehicle for getting the case to the appellate court for a ruling on the admissibility of DNA testing. If it were ruled inadmissible, then the defendant would receive a new trial without evidence of a DNA match. In this case, which turned out to be a highly publicized landmark one, the Supreme Judicial Court approved DNA testing as admissible in criminal trial proceedings.

The widely heralded appellate opinion carried my name as the trial judge and for some time judges and lawyers congratulated me for helping to establish a law for all times in the Commonwealth.

In another noteworthy case, a prisoner who had served twenty years for murder was granted a new trial by another judge who courageously found that the man had not been properly convicted and that it was unlikely that he was guilty. The government was given an opportunity to retry the man and when the parties appeared in court before me, the prosecutor announced that the defendant would not be retried. I therefore dismissed the case and released the man on the request of his lawyer with no objection from the prosecutor. He has been doing well in the community as a youth counselor for well over a decade. To this day, many people see me as the person who cured a terrible injustice when I ordered his release.

Persnickety to the Point of Exasperation

A reservation clerk for a major airline at Logan Airport in Boston received an anonymous telephone call disclosing that two black men took the airline's shuttle that morning to New York, were returning on the 3 PM or 4 PM shuttle, and one of them would be carrying a large amount of heroin in the crotch of his pants. The caller also said that one of the men was named Donald Williams, he was approximately five feet six inches tall, and would be wearing a black baseball cap.

The clerk notified the state police and two troopers met the shuttle at the gate. The last two passengers to leave the plane fit the caller's description. The defendant was not the one wearing the black baseball cap, but he had a noticeable bulge on the left side of his crotch. The two men moved slowly, scanning the area, and frequently looked at one of the troopers. They were met by two other men and then the defendant walked away quickly from the group to the upper terminal, bypassing the baggage claim. One trooper followed and asked him if he would speak with him and the defendant agreed. He provided the trooper with his name, but could produce no identification. When asked about the bulge, the defendant did not respond. The trooper frisked him and determined that the bulge was a hard object about the size of a cigarette pack. He removed it and found packages of tightly wrapped heroin.

The defendant claimed the police action was illegal because the police had no way of knowing if the informant was reliable and had a basis for his information. The prosecution responded that those considerations were overridden by the police corroboration of the informant's information as well as the nature of the suspicious bulge and the man's conduct. The experienced trooper testified that drug couriers do not check luggage. I ruled that the stop, inquiry, frisk, and arrest were warranted on the quantum of information possessed by the officer.

The Supreme Judicial Court, in a six-to-one decision, reversed my ruling, stating the police lacked "probable cause" because the corroboration and conduct by the defendant were inadequate to justify the police contact.[24]

The one dissenting justice wrote, "The court today is persnickety to the point of exasperation in its demands on the police."

---

[24] *Commonwealth v. Spence*, 403 Mass. 179 (1988).

Logan Airport

One of a Kind

In a small claims case, the plaintiff claimed that the dry cleaner had damaged his $750 custom-made suit purchased in Italy five years before. The dry cleaner acknowledged the slight discoloration and offered to pay $35 while the customer wanted the $750 replacement cost. Neither was a lawyer and neither understood that the dry cleaner was seeking to pay traditional tort damages measured as the diminished value of the property while the customer was seeking specialized "Trinity Church" damages. Years later, I again dealt with this issue in a notable pier renovation case.

The company was renovating a wooden pier and platform that were central to a new waterfront park in Boston. Their workers used welding torches in high wind conditions, causing creosote to catch fire and destroy much of the pier. The plaintiff Port Authority sued the company, which took the position that, if it were negligent, the damages should be limited to the diminishment in market value of the pier due to the fire. That sum would have been just a fraction of the cost of either building a new pier or repairing the damaged pier, over one million dollars. People don't buy and sell piers very often, so, unlike the automobile market, there is no marketplace to value undamaged and damaged used piers. I instructed the jury that they could try to compute the diminishment in value due to the defendant's negligence but if they could not, they could look to repair, replacement, and renovation costs.

The jury found they could not assess the market value of the pier before and after the fire. I was relieved because a diminution in market value would not have been a fair assessment of the loss. A pier is a "one of a kind" property, sort of like a custom-made suit. The verdict that exceeded one million dollars was more in the spirit of rebuilding, repairing, or renovating the structure. My alternative damage instruction was supported by the famous "Trinity Church" case where the court found that the damage to the very unique church building could not be measured in terms of diminishment in its market value.[25] The construction company appealed and the Supreme Judicial Court affirmed my rulings.[26]

---

[25] *Trinity Church in the City of Boston v. John Hancock Mutual Life Ins. Co.*, 399 Mass. 43 (1987).
[26] *Mass. Port Authority v. Sciaba Construction Corporation*, 54 Mass. Appt. Ct. 509 (2002).

Years later, I accompanied a group of visiting foreign judges on a cruise of Boston Harbor. When we came within sight of the pier, I tried to describe the case through an interpreter. On reflection, had I owned and been wearing a custom-made suit, I might have made myself better understood through an analogy.

Trinity Church
Copley Square, Boston

A Big If

I, along with every first-year law student, studied the 350-year-old English case of *Tuberville v. Savage* where, in response to a slight from Savage, Tuberville placed his hand on his sword handle and uttered the immortal words, "*If* it were not for assize-time, I would not take this language from you."[27] Savage then attacked and injured Tuberville, who sued him. Savage's defense was that he acted in response to an assault and threat. The court ruled that a conditional threat is neither a threat nor an assault and Tuberville therefore won the case. How many times do we say to our children or grandchildren, "*If* you weren't so cute, I would punish you"? Under the law, that is not a threat.

In a contract case where I was presiding, the plaintiff had received a bad check from the defendant. He did not sue him within the six-year statute of limitations. After a decade, he finally made a demand on the defendant for the money owed and the defendant responded with a letter stating that he would search his files and *if* it turned out that he owed the money, then he would pay it. He paid nothing and the plaintiff sued claiming that the letter was a new promise.

I dismissed the case, ruling that the defendant had made a conditional promise and not a binding contract that might resuscitate the expired claim. The plaintiff appealed to the Appellate Division of the District Court and then again to the Supreme Judicial Court, which affirmed my decision, applying my reasoning.[28]

The two-letter word *if* makes things conditional and usually renders them unenforceable.

---

[27] *Tuberville v. Savage*, King's Bench, 86 Eng. Rep. 684 (1669). Assize-time was the scheduled sitting of the court session in that locale.
[28] *Epstein v. Seigel*, 396 Mass. 278 (1985).

My Three Strikes

When sentencing the defendant for unarmed bank robbery after a jury trial, the defendant presented himself as a mixed bag. He had a record of criminal convictions related to alcohol and drugs. He was middle aged, appeared intelligent and articulate, and expressed a real desire to address his substance abuse issues. I imposed a sentence of four to five years in prison that was on the low end of the sentencing guidelines given his prior criminal record.

As to his offense, when committing the bank robbery, the man was wearing a distinctive red baseball cap that he dropped in the vicinity of the bank. The police recovered the cap and arrested him after a tip from a family friend. DNA was extracted from the hat by one state police chemist and from the man's saliva by a second chemist.

At trial, those chemists did not testify, but their supervisor did. The defendant was found guilty. The Appeals Court reversed the conviction, ruling that the supervising chemist did not have sufficient contact with the analyses of the two testing chemists.[29] The trial occurred years before the landmark US Supreme Court case that essentially made the testimony of analyzing chemists mandatory at trial.[30]

A new trial was ordered. The defendant pled guilty before another judge and received a reduced sentence as the government's case had weakened.

When the defendant was released from prison he was placed on probation. He continued to struggle with his demons, especially alcohol, and the probation department sought revocation of his probation several times for violation of probation conditions.

Against the advice of the probation officer, I returned the man to a probationary status with new treatment conditions a number of times. Once, I sent him to prison for a short period and wrote, "The Court hopes and expects that the defendant will avail himself of alcohol and other self-improvement programs in the institution and be awarded the program good time for such efforts." Another time, I reduced a short sentence by one month and wrote: "It is hoped that the Court's action will be an incentive for the defendant to seek out

---

[29] *Commonwealth v. Dexter*, 75 Mass. App. Ct. 1110 (2009).
[30] *Melendez-Diaz v. Massachusetts*, 129 S.Ct. 2527 (2009).

community assistance for his alcohol and substance abuse issues and will dedicate himself to living within the law."

The probation officer who had hands-on experience with the man knew otherwise and advised me that, as to him, "a tiger does not change its stripes." I thought I knew the defendant's true potential. Our worlds collided when the defendant was arrested and again convicted of robbery and sentenced to six years in prison.

For the defendant, that probably was his sixth strike. For me, perhaps it was only my third: my assessment of him at sentencing, my misplaced optimism in the face of his probation violations, and my not heeding the advice of those who worked in the trenches. We all do live and learn, even late in life.

Sex, Lies, and Arson

The law looks askance at attempts by law enforcement to use trickery or deception to elicit a confession from a suspect. I have always been amused by the story of a case from Bucks County, Pennsylvania, where the police had the suspect put his hand on a Xerox machine while answering a question and then printed out a paper with the words "not the truth." The suspect then confessed. The court threw out the confession. Many of the closer cases deal with the police encouraging a confession with a false or misleading statement, for example, erroneously suggesting that the suspect's companion had already confessed and had implicated the suspect. The case before me was even closer.

The police were investigating the arson of a boat that was on a trailer outside the victim's house. The defendant lived next door to the victim and both their homes faced the lake. The fire happened while the defendant was hosting a party at his home.

One week later, the police fire investigator interviewed the defendant at the fire station. The defendant denied setting the fire and when asked about who might have set it, the defendant responded that he suspected it had to do with the victim's homosexual activities. When asked to elaborate, the defendant said he would discuss the victim's gay activities "off the record" and the officer agreed. He then, in an increasingly agitated and angry manner, described explicit sexual conduct between men that was visible from the defendant's house and yard. The defendant reported that his son was reluctant to spend time at the lake house. The defendant said that he was "fucking pissed" about what was happening in the victim's yard.

These "off the record" statements were not included in the defendant's signed statement, but the prosecution sought to introduce the oral statements at trial. After an evidentiary hearing, I admitted the statements on grounds that there was no police coercion that in any way compelled the man to utter incriminating statements.[31]

The defendant was convicted at trial and he appealed. The Appeals Court found no error in my admitting the statements and affirmed the conviction. The Supreme Judicial Court elected to review the decision of the Appeals Court and affirmed the conviction by a

---

[31] It was also learned that the defendant told another partygoer that he changed his shirt during the evening because he had spilled gasoline on himself.

vote of three to two with a very strong dissent.[32] The Supreme Judicial Court ruled that law enforcement must exercise caution when employing deceit or trickery or when giving assurances to a suspect. They found here that the defendant's oral statements were all voluntary. The dissenting judges felt I had erred by not holding the police to their "off the record" promises.

The police conduct was troubling to me because they should have explained to the defendant at the time what "off the record" would mean in this situation.

---

[32] *Commonwealth v. Tremblay*, 77 Mass. App. Ct 318 (2010), 460 Mass. 199 (2011).

Appealed Early and Often

Mabel Greineder was murdered around Thanksgiving of 1999 and her husband was tried and convicted of her murder in June of 2001. After the verdict, the case was before the Supreme Judicial Court three times and was before the United States Supreme Court twice. It's finally over with, I think. I thought that five appellate reviews must be a record and now I remember a sixth appellate review, right at the start of trial.[33]

Jury selection was completed and the jurors, attorneys, and I took a bus trip to Morse's Pond for a view of the places that would be referred to by the witnesses during the trial. We were going to start the formal trial proceedings the next day. There was an issue to be resolved before the attorneys' opening statements. The defense attorney wanted to include the fact that there were two unsolved murders of women in the general vicinity of Wellesley at the time of the instant killing, the inference being that there was a serial killer lurking and that the husband was innocent. The government asserted that there was no evidence, only defense speculation of a serial murderer.

I ruled that the defense attorney could cite the multiple murders at the time, but only for the limited proposition that the police erroneously jumped to the conclusion that the husband was the murderer. For example, upon arriving at the scene of the crime, they interviewed the husband, who had called the police, but neglected to instruct other officers to watch for suspicious persons in and around the reservation surrounding the pond. The defense felt I erred in not giving them *carte blanche* in discussing the other murders, while the government felt I erred and that they would be seriously prejudiced by my ruling that gave the defense limited permission. In a very unusual procedure, the government sought appellate review of my ruling on an emergency basis from the Supreme Judicial Court. I believe that the attorneys wrote briefs, submitted them to the appellate court, drove ten or twelve miles to Boston, and made their arguments in the evening. I did not learn of this appeal until I arrived at court the next morning to start the trial.

The justice of the Supreme Judicial Court assigned to hear emergency matters sent his ruling to me first thing in the morning. He declined to overrule any aspect of my ruling.

---

[33] *Commonwealth v. Greineder*, 464 Mass. 580 (2013).

Give Me a Brake

The auto accident case was an "open and shut" one by the time the plaintiff finished presenting his evidence and I granted the defendant's motion for a directed verdict. The plaintiff appealed and the Appeals Court reversed my decision and ordered a new trial.

The plaintiff sped through a stop sign at a T intersection without slowing down and rammed the vehicle approaching from his right. There was evidence that trees or bushes obstructed the plaintiff's view. The plaintiff claimed that the defendant was at fault because he was going too fast and/or did not slow down at the intersection. We are a "comparative negligence" state where a plaintiff driver in an accident case cannot prevail and recover any amount if he or she is more than 50% at fault.

I reasoned that, even if the defendant were speeding or did not slow at the intersection, which he denied, the plaintiff, by his own admissions, had to be at least 51% at fault. The Appeals Court ruled that my granting of a directed verdict was not appropriate because there were facts in dispute. My decision was reversed and the case was remanded for a new trial.

I received a friendly phone call from the judge on the Appeals Court who had written the decision reversing my ruling. He agreed that the plaintiff's case was one of the weakest he had seen, yet because it was fact-driven, the plaintiff had a right to have the jury pick and choose from the evidence. I told him a new jury would deliberate for only two minutes. It turned out I was wrong. The jury deliberated for ten minutes before finding against the plaintiff.

This low-stakes case teaches that judges should stick with the law and let the jury stick with the facts.

<u>Going Up?</u>

I avoid elevators, not because I see them as unsafe, but taking the stairs offers a healthy alternative. When passing up an elevator, I am often reminded of an unforgettable case, one with novel medical–legal issues.

The plaintiff was an office worker at the John Hancock Tower in Boston's Copley Square. Six years earlier, she was diagnosed with multiple sclerosis, but had symptoms so mild that the disease was considered in remission. She tripped and fell when exiting Elevator 27 when it stopped two to three inches below the lobby floor. It appeared at the time that she suffered only minor bruising. The next day, her multiple sclerosis symptoms significantly worsened. By the time of trial years later, she was dependent upon crutches and her workweek had been reduced to twelve hours.

The plaintiff had sued the elevator company and the court was confronted with the novel issue of whether mild trauma could exacerbate multiple sclerosis. Medical experts held polar views on the subject. The plaintiff's expert, a neurologist at the Beth Israel Hospital who specialized in the treatment of multiple sclerosis, testified that physical trauma can alter the blood brain barrier and disrupt a sheath and impair the flow of nerve impulses from the brain to the body. Two defense expert neurologists testified that those views were unsubstantiated and not generally accepted in the medical community. The Multiple Sclerosis Society takes the position that trauma does not affect the progress of the disease. The jury found that the defendant elevator company was negligent in its maintenance and repair of Elevator 27, but that the accident did not cause the exacerbation of the plaintiff's multiple sclerosis.

The plaintiff appealed, claiming I did not instruct the jury correctly according to brand new standards for assessing expert testimony. The defendant also appealed, claiming I should not have admitted the plaintiff's expert testimony in the first place.

The Appeals Court found that my instructions were appropriate including those on the exacerbation of a previously existing injury. Because the verdict against the plaintiff was affirmed, the Appeals Court decided not to address the issues raised by the defendant.[34]

---

[34] *Louise Higgins v. Delta Elevator Service Corporation*, 45 Mass. App. Ct. 643 (1998).

The medical board had disciplined the plaintiff's expert neurologist because he prescribed a narcotic drug to his nurse although the rules forbid physicians from prescribing certain drugs to employees and family members. I would not allow the defense to smear the physician by bringing to the jury's attention an administrative sanction for a minor misdeed that did not rise to the level of criminal conduct.

The defendant's attorney also sought to bar the neurologist from testifying that the fall caused an exacerbation of the illness. I ruled that the neurologist's "blood-brain" theory was not "junk science" and should be considered by the jury. I allowed him to testify, knowing that there were judges in other jurisdictions who had barred neurologists, including this one, from testifying on that issue.

It's unfortunate that the appellate court declined to deal with the most interesting issues in the case, which included impeachment of an expert who has received an administrative punishment and whether the theory that multiple sclerosis can be exacerbated by mild trauma was junk science.

Present elevator bank at the John Hancock Tower
now known as 200 Clarendon

Pork Chow Mein, Anyone?

The jury lunched on pizza and cold cuts during the murder trial. As a precautionary measure, I wanted them in the courthouse rather than in the community over the lunch hour. It was a difficult case and I decided to reward them with a quality lunch, so I instructed the court officers to order gourmet Chinese food. They did, and the bill was over $300 whereas the bill on the other days for pizza or cold cuts was only about $60. I kidded the court officers telling them that we could be indicted for wasting government money and would have to wait out the seven-year statute of limitations before we were in the clear. For years we counted down the time and planned a "freedom day" at the expiration of the seven years.

There are times when a statute of limitations seems unfair; where a severely injured motorist can't bring suit after expiration of the three-year period for torts, or where a vulnerable person can't sue a deadbeat debtor after the six-year period for contracts expires. Nevertheless, it's probably good public policy to "draw a line in the sand" so people can get on with the rest of their lives.

Consider this case. The father died leaving his farm to his eight children. Alden, the eldest son, paid cash to six of his siblings in exchange for their shares. The remaining sibling, Leona, declined to sell her share and instead insisted on exchanging her one-eighth share for "the knoll in the hog field" where she planned to build a house. Alden orally agreed. I referred to the knoll as "Pig Hill." Leona didn't want an immediate conveyance because she was having marital difficulties and was reducing her marital estate. Twenty years passed before she finally told Alden to convey the knoll to her. He refused, saying that she gave up her rights to the knoll and he would pay her what he paid the other siblings. She sued.

The applicable statute of limitations was six years, but it was impossible to know when the initial breach occurred, probably during some confrontation within the twenty years. My research uncovered an appellate case where, in a commercial setting, the court ruled that twenty years of inaction was an excessive period for an oral contract for land and that the right to the property was forfeited. I so ruled in this case, finding that Leona had forfeited her right to the specific parcel of land. She appealed. My decision was reversed as the appellate court ruled that rights should not be forfeited after twenty years where the oral agreement is within a family setting.[35]

Unfortunately, the appellate court did not give us guidance as to how many years would have to pass before rights would be forfeited nor did they rule on what would have happened if Leona had died and her heir wanted to build on the property. So, my error provides only limited guidance to future generations of those who would want to live on their own "Pig Hill."

---

[35] *Leona Fox Barber v. Alden E. Fox*, 36 Mass. App. Ct. 525 (1994).

Only an Inch

An inch or less has made the difference in World Series and Super Bowl play as well as in potentially fatal accidents and missed opportunities. For example, before surgery, my aortic heart valve had the diameter of a fraction of an inch, that of a pencil lead, and, had it gotten any smaller, there might have been no "Bench Notes" and no me.

The defendant was wearing a backpack containing a large kitchen knife with its handle sticking out of the top by an inch. That inch turned out to make all the difference. The defendant had agreed to meet with a police officer to discuss a police investigation in which he was a suspect. It was the officer's intention to arrest him on a warrant at their meeting.

When they met at the location the defendant had chosen, he tried to steer the officer to a dark and remote area. When proceeding in that direction, other officers appeared and arrested the man. The investigating officer might have been in real danger because the protruding knife was easily accessible to the defendant without having to remove his backpack. Although it is not a crime to simply possess or carry a kitchen knife, there is a law that forbids one from "using" a knife in a manner that can cause serious harm.[36]

I ruled that the jury had sufficient evidence to consider whether the defendant broke the law. The jury convicted him and he appealed.

The Appeals Court found that, when protruding one inch, the knife was easily accessible and "usable" and, under the circumstances, it was capable of causing serious harm. They affirmed the conviction.[37]

I guess it can be said that I was upheld on appeal by an inch.

---

[36] General Laws c. 269, § 10(b): The statute forbids a person being arrested on a warrant from having on his person a dangerous weapon. It carries with it a judicial limitation that the weapon must be used in a manner that has the capacity to cause serious harm.

[37] *Commonwealth v. Bradshaw*, 86 Mass. App. Ct. 74 (2014).

Doing Right Can Be Wrong

The narrator in Robert Frost's "After Apple Picking" is exhausted when he quits picking apples and tries to doze off. His sleep is disturbed by a seemingly senseless rule that renders worthless any apple that is dropped and touches the ground as it must be discarded and sent to the cider heap whether bruised or not. I am also disturbed by arbitrary rules.

A plaintiff who sues an out-of-state driver because of an auto accident is required by law to serve the legal papers on the Registrar of Motor Vehicles and immediately send a copy of the documents by registered mail to the other driver, who usually forwards them to his insurance company because it will defend him.[38]

In such an accident case before me, the plaintiff's lawyer correctly served the Registrar but notified the out-of-state driver's insurance company directly in writing rather than forwarding the documents to the insured person. The other driver's lawyer provided by the insurance company moved to dismiss the lawsuit because the documents had not been sent directly to his client as the law requires. The lawyer agreed with me that, had his client received the legal papers, he would have turned them over to the insurance company so that no one was prejudiced by the attorney's mistake. The lawyer maintained that, nevertheless, the action had to be dismissed because the plaintiff's attorney did not follow the rules.

I felt badly for the plaintiff's attorney as he was not experienced in civil matters and he had been ill around the time of these transactions. Rather than dismiss the case, I allowed plaintiff's counsel leave to send the papers to the other driver, who would undoubtedly forward them to the lawyer provided by the insurance company.

My refusal to dismiss the case was appealed. The Appeals Court reversed my ruling in a rather curt decision stating that I did not have the discretion to bend the rules.[39]

In retrospect, the appellate court was right in bringing me up short. If I were permitted the discretion to ignore established rules in order to help someone in need, what would prevent another decision maker from ignoring the rules in order to disadvantage someone? In the play "A Man for All Seasons," William Roper tells Sir Thomas More

---

[38] General Laws c. 90, § 3c.
[39] *Mark Hanson v. Daniel Venditelli et al*, 47 Mass. App. Ct. 413 (1999).

that he would cut down all of the laws in England to get at the Devil. More's response is that, without the laws, Roper would have nowhere to hide when the Devil turned 'round on him. So, occasionally an unbruised apple goes to the cider heap in an effort to prevent inferior apples from going to market.

Whether to Trump or Not to Trump, That Is the Question

It's enough to give a trial judge a headache when there are two conflicting laws that tell the judge to proceed in opposite directions. Should the judge rule that one law trumps the other or instead try to harmonize or balance them? At the time of a trial before me, an issue of this nature remained unresolved because our highest state court had recently been equally divided on it. I ruled that one statute should trump the other and the Supreme Judicial Court later reversed me with two justices dissenting.[40]

A woman's boyfriend dropped her off at a local bar and intended to pick her up later in the evening. The defendant was a bar patron at the time. When she left the bar to call her boyfriend, the defendant followed her into the street. The woman claimed that he pulled her into a basement stairwell and raped her. The defendant claimed that the woman was a prostitute who agreed to sex for money and didn't complain until he refused to pay her.

At trial, the complaining witness testified. The defense attorney sought to bring to the jury's attention the fact that the woman had a record for prostitution that included a recent conviction.

One law permits an attorney to impeach or confront a witness with a criminal conviction that meets certain criteria relating to time frame, severity, and penalty. Here the conviction would qualify. Another law known as the "Rape Shield Law" precludes evidence of the reputation of a witness or of specific acts by the witness relating to sexual conduct. There are some exceptions to this rule that do not apply here. The Rape Shield Law grew out of the vilification over the years of women who complain of sexual assault. I ruled that the Rape Shield law trumps the law of impeachment as a matter of both public policy and legislative intent and that it would not be appropriate for me to balance the merits of each statute in the context of the specific case. Therefore, the jury never learned that the complainant had a record for prostitution. The defendant was convicted of aggravated rape and he appealed. The Supreme Judicial Court disagreed with my ruling and found, 5-2, that the trial judge must consider the evidence in the particular case and exercise discretion after balancing the purposes of the Rape Shield statute with the probative value of the prostitution conviction. This balancing is a harmonizing of the statutes.

---

[40] *Commonwealth v. Harris*, 443 Mass. 714 (2005).

When I learned that a new trial was ordered, I felt badly that the complainant would have to face another painful jury trial. I later learned that she was spared a retrial because the defendant pled guilty to reduced charges and received a sentence of time served. I am not bothered when a murder, robbery, burglary, or drug case has to be retried. It's the retrial of sexual assault and other cases with vulnerable witnesses that troubles me.

Making a Mountain Out of a Molehill

After almost twenty-five years, I finally understand the appellate decision in this criminal case, I think. Within most serious crimes are lesser ones. For example, a person who steals a bicycle worth over $250 is guilty of grand larceny, but if the evidence at trial indicates that the bicycle was worth less than $250, then the person can be convicted of the lesser included offense of petit larceny.

I thought I had a similar situation where a man was charged with choking a woman who, fortunately, got away. The statute makes it a crime when one *attempts to commit murder by poisoning, drowning, or strangling another.*[41] I instructed the jury that the crime required proof that the defendant physically choked the victim in a failed attempt to kill her and, if there was insufficient proof that he attempted to kill her, then the jury could find him guilty of assault and battery, which is defined as a harmful touching. The jury convicted the man of that lesser crime and I sentenced him to one year in jail followed by one year of probation. He appealed and I was reversed, well, sort of.

The Appeals Court first found that I was wrong in requiring proof that the crime required a touching.[42] It ruled that "poisoning, drowning, or strangling" modified "murder" and not "attempts." In a footnote, the appellate court gave a theoretical example as to how that might be accomplished where a perpetrator sneaks up behind a victim with a garroting cord and is interrupted as he puts his arms over the victim's head. They reasoned that since the statute could be violated without a touching, then the crime of assault and battery was not a lesser included crime because it required a touching. They ruled that the conviction in my case should be for the lesser crime of "assault," which does not require a touching. Since the crimes of "assault" and "assault and battery" carry the same punishment, the case turned out to be a rather Pyrrhic victory for the defendant.

The technicalities, theories, and the forced example looked to me like counting the number of angels that can dance on the head of a pin. I defy anyone to understand the appellate opinion on a first or second reading. Look how long it took me.

---

[41] Massachusetts General Laws, c. 265, § 16.
[42] *Commonwealth v. Dixon*, 34 Mass. App. Ct. 653 (1993).

Not Bad and Not Good

When running with my ten-year-old grandson Rayan on the Washington & Old Dominion Trail in Virginia, he ran so fast that I quickly lost sight of him. I later commented that Rayan's running was "not bad," which, of course, meant "very good." When my wife Lynn described my haircut as "not good," she probably meant "pretty bad." In a very troublesome case, I had to reckon with such definitions in the technical world of commercial banking and the Uniform Commercial Code.

The comptroller of a foreign motors dealership embezzled hundreds of thousands of dollars from his employer through two fraudulent schemes involving the bank that serviced the employer with auto loans on a daily basis. The bank sued the foreign motors company on loans that were not paid off because of the embezzlement. The foreign motors company sued the bank on their handling of checks deposited and withdrawn by the company's rogue employee who was then in prison for his crimes. The complex litigation amounted to warfare that raged for over twenty years in the Superior Court and Appeals Court. I conducted two trials in the Superior Court and another judge conducted a third on matters left after the appeal.

A threshold issue in my trials was whether or not the bank acted in bad faith in regard to certain transactions. The Code under which the case was tried provided little guidance as to what constitutes "bad faith." I remember the polar advice that I received from the lawyers. The bank's lawyers pressed me for a very narrow definition of what it means to act in bad faith as they wanted the smallest target possible for their client. I remember glibly thinking to myself that they wanted it limited to acts of terror. On the other hand, the lawyers representing the foreign motors dealership wanted the broadest definition for bad faith to provide the jury with a huge target. I was tempted to ask them if having overdue library books qualified.

Although the Code does not define "bad faith," there is a comment section in the Code suggesting bad faith is an "absence of good faith," something like my "not good" haircut.

I gave the jury a number of negative factors they could consider in assessing whether there was bad faith. At one end of the spectrum I included negligence, recklessness, and commercially unreasonable conduct and, on the other end, I offered the more traditional language from fraud cases incorporating dishonesty, acting in self-interest, and knowingly doing wrong. Since both sides were totally dissatisfied with my instruction on bad faith, I thought it had a chance of withstanding an appeal. I was wrong, it didn't.

The Appeals Court examined both in-state and out-of-state legal precedent and ruled that my definition of bad faith was too broad.[43] They ruled that I should have limited it to "conscious and deliberate decision-making on the part of the bank that enabled the fraud by the embezzler."

I wonder if the Appeals Court thought I was "not bad," "not good," or somewhere in between as the trial judge on such a complex and difficult case.

---

[43] *Bank of America v. Prestige Imports, Inc.*, 75 Mass. App. Ct. 741 (2009).

Knock, Knock. Who's There?

A "no knock" warrant authorizes the police to force open a door and enter a home or office without knocking or identifying themselves and their purpose. This type of warrant is reserved for situations where it is likely that someone within might destroy evidence, such as flushing drugs down the toilet. Most warrants must be executed under the "knock and announce rule," which requires both a knocking by the police and the announcing of their authority and purpose. Simply barging in can present a physical danger to both the surprised occupants and the police. Failure to follow the terms of the warrant might result in the judicial suppression of the evidence uncovered in the search.

The police had a "knock and announce" warrant to search a first-floor apartment in Somerville that was occupied by two sisters. One of the officers had coached the sisters during their school years and knew of their interest in sports. The police knocked on the door and a female voice asked who was there. An officer said "Somerville Pop Warner" as a ruse that they were civilians collecting for local football. An occupant opened the door and then tried to close it when she saw it was the police. The police then forced their way while announcing their purpose. The women were charged with drug trafficking after the police recovered drugs, paraphernalia, and money. In court they sought to suppress the seized evidence.

I ordered the evidence suppressed, finding that the police violated the terms of the "knock and announce" search warrant by using a ruse to induce an occupant to open the door. The prosecution appealed my ruling to the Appeals Court and the appeal was transferred to the Supreme Judicial Court, which apparently felt the issue was an important one.

The highest court found that I had erred and they reversed my ruling. Their decision stated that a consensual entry, even if obtained by a ruse or trickery does not violate the rule especially because there was no likelihood of violence, no intrusion on privacy, and no damage to property.[44]

I have always been troubled in cases where the police use a ruse to gain an advantage.

---

[44] *Commonwealth v. Darlene and Denise Goggin*, 412 Mass. 200 (1992).

If the Creek Don't Rise[45]

I reminded a witness from West Virginia that he must return to court to complete his testimony. He said he would return, "if the creek don't rise." The creek always seems to rise when I try to enforce a judicial order or court rule. People often seek more time than allowed by the court by attempting to show that the other side has done something that made the task impossible to complete within the time frame.

Rule 36 of the Massachusetts Rules of Criminal Procedure requires that a person facing a criminal charge be tried within one year. That time period can be extended when the defendant is responsible for periods of delay.

Three defendants were charged with aggravated rape. They allegedly offered a ride to a male and female and ejected the male from the vehicle and later raped the female and tried to run her over. The defendants were arrested and were released on bail so that they were at liberty in the community awaiting trial. Over twenty months passed and they were yet to be tried. Their lawyers sought dismissal of the charges.

I heard the defendants' motions and ruled that, in this case, there were time periods that had to be deducted from the twenty months that included those periods where the defendants caused the delay by asking for continuances, by filing motions to be heard at later hearings, and by requesting funds to engage the services of a defense investigator. I also ruled that time periods where the defendants acquiesced to the passage of time had to be deducted too, as when they neither complained nor sought action from a judge who had yet to rule on some pending motions. I noted that the defendants' motions were made less compelling because they were at liberty awaiting trial and, in cases of this nature, delay almost always works to benefit the defendants as some witnesses move away and the memories of others (and their desire to appear in court) fade.

I performed the time calculations for the periods where the defendants caused the delay and for the periods in which they acquiesced and probably benefitted from the delay. I found that the one-year period had not legally expired. The defendants appealed and the Appeals Court reversed my ruling, finding that I had erred. The

---

[45] From the song, "If the Lord's Willing and the Creek Don't Rise" by Jerry Reed and popularized by Johnny Cash.

prosecution then further appealed and the Supreme Judicial Court reversed the Appeals Court and reinstituted my decision.[46]

So, from the standpoint of the prosecution, the delay and acquiescence by the defense tolled or extended the one-year period and gave them more time, just as if the creek had risen.

---

[46] *Commonwealth v. Lauria*, 411 Mass. 63 (1991).

A Higher Law

Thirty-nine people descended on the Draper Laboratories in Cambridge, Massachusetts, one morning to hand leaflets to employees and others declaring that the laboratory's work on government projects facilitated the nuclear arms race. The plant security officers told the group to leave because they were trespassing. All but four of the demonstrators left the property. They were given a final chance to leave by the local police and were arrested and charged with trespassing when they again refused.

The jury trial for the four demonstrators was quite a scene as their supporters were in the courtroom, the public corridors, and outside the courthouse with placards. Interesting issues were raised about the competing harms doctrine contrasting the harm of trespassing with that of nuclear destruction. The jury found the defendants guilty. The government recommended a short period of incarceration because they were repeat illegal protesters. I felt that a fine was more appropriate. With a courtroom full of supporters, the defendants said they would rather go to jail than pay a fine. I did not want them to appear as martyrs so I sent them home to think about their decision.

When they returned days later to a near-empty courtroom, three of them still insisted that they "work off the fine" in jail and were taken into custody. One of them sent me a story about a judge in a similar case who visited the demonstrator in jail and they subsequently fell in love. They appealed and, surprisingly, the Supreme Judicial Court took the case from the Appeals Court.

The most unforgettable part of the case was the rendering of the jury verdict itself. The jury indicated that they had a verdict and a statement. The prosecutor advised that I should not accept the statement because the standard instruction at the start of the case is that the jury is to render a verdict "and say no more." I disagreed. I felt that the jury needed a catharsis after this emotional trial. The foreman read a note stating,

> *These findings are based on a narrow interpretation of the law. We feel that there are important philosophical and perhaps moral questions that transcend the scope of this trial. We feel they should be debated in the broadest possible forum.*

The Supreme Judicial Court affirmed the convictions.[47] As to the foreman's note, the defense position was that the jury did not find the defendants guilty beyond a reasonable doubt. The Supreme Judicial Court ruled that the note, in fact, was an affirmation that they had indeed found guilt according to the appropriate legal standard.

In retrospect, I feel good about the case and the people involved. I saw the defendants as well-meaning people who felt their cause would best be served with a period of confinement. In that sense, they probably saw me as an obstacle. I have enormous respect for the jurors, who took the case very seriously and had the courage to explain their discomfort in returning the appropriate verdict. The prosecutor went on to become a premier assistant district attorney.[48] The case came early in my judicial career and served as a good learning experience.

---

[47] *Commonwealth v. Paul Hood,* 389 Mass. 581 (1983).
[48] Assistant District Attorney Adrienne Lynch has been a close friend and colleague over the years.

Deception by Government

During political campaigns we seldom take things at face value. All candidates exaggerate their positives and minimize their negatives and do the reverse for their opponents. Also, during campaign season, we show some tolerance for misrepresentations and even outright fabrications. Although the perjury laws cover all persons who take an oath to tell the truth, it's generally accepted that a guilty person will deny culpability under oath and that people stretch the truth for a legal cause. In nearly forty years of judging, I tried only one perjury case. Should we give law enforcement a pass in its quest to convict the criminal? I try not to do so but am the first to admit that I may lack consistency.

In the *Goggin* case (on page 61), I showed little tolerance for the "Pop Warner" ruse the police used to gain entrance to the drug dealers' home. However, in the *Tremblay* case (on pages 45–46), I tolerated the ruse by the officer who said that the defendant could speak to him "off the record." Two other confession cases also come to mind.

In the first, the defendant was questioned by the police while being treated in the emergency room following an automobile accident. He was facing immediate surgery for a dislocated hip and an injury to his mouth. The investigating officer knew, but did not disclose to the defendant, that someone had died in the accident, nor did the officer explain to the defendant that he had a right not to consent to a blood test. The man was subsequently charged with motor vehicle homicide and operating a vehicle under the influence of alcohol. I ruled that the ruse of withholding the fact that it was a fatal accident and failing to disclose that the man could decline to take the blood test made his statement and the testing not consensual. I suppressed the evidence, the government appealed, and the appellate court agreed with me.[49]

In the second case, a fire in a building killed two residents. Investigators interviewed the defendant twice on the day of the fire. Four days later the man voluntarily went to the police station for another interview. They spoke in a relaxed setting where the man had cigarette breaks, coffee, and cold beverages. After several hours, he made some admissions. When he said that he wanted to leave, the police disclosed that an arrest warrant had been obtained before his

---

[49] *Commonwealth v. Angivone*, 383 Mass. 30 (1981).

arrival at the station. That ruse had led the man to believe he was free to leave during the interview.

The man was charged with murder and I heard the motion to suppress the statements. I ruled that the ruse had no impact on the voluntariness of the defendant's statements. He was convicted of second-degree murder and appealed.

The Appeals Court upheld the conviction and was not troubled by what they concluded was a valid confession.[50]

Although the appellate courts agreed with me in both cases, I'm not sure that I applied the law consistently.

---

[50] *Commonwealth v. Robinson*, 78 Mass. App. Ct. 633 (2010).

Past and Future Patterns

People who are charged with committing a crime often have a history of past misconduct. Facing a trial, an accused defendant is presumed to be innocent. It wouldn't be fair to bring up his past because the jury might think that if he did something bad before, he probably did something bad again. So, past misconduct is generally not admissible.

There is an exception that deals with patterns. Remember the "Pink Panther" film where the thief always left a pink glove at the scene of each of his thefts? Well, if the thief were being tried for the latest theft involving a pink glove, evidence of his involvement with similar pink glove thefts would be admissible to establish a pattern. I presided over a trial where there was the novel issue as to whether future misdeeds can prove a pattern.

In a sordid case, the adult defendant allegedly plied four teenage girls with alcohol and drugs before he sexually molested each of them when they were asleep or semi-conscious. After his arrest, he was released on bail to live with his sister.

Within three months, the man convinced his teenage nephew to recruit a teenage girl and her friend to come to the sister's house at night, enter through a window, consume alcohol and drugs, engage in sex with them, and leave before the sister woke up. The man even put the plan in writing for his nephew. Nothing came of the plan because the nephew was unable to reach the girl.

At the rape trial, the prosecution sought to admit the note and conversation with the nephew to prove a pattern. The defendant's attorney vehemently objected, claiming that it was like a "nuclear bomb." I ruled that future bad acts are admissible to show a pattern where those acts were of an identical nature and occurred shortly after the crime occurred for which he was being tried. The defendant was convicted. He appealed and the case was affirmed.[51]

I thought the issue was so novel and so sensitive that it would engender a lengthy decision by the Appeals Court followed by further review by the Supreme Judicial Court. Not so, as the Appeals Court merely stated that, "Whether the acts occurred before or after the acts for which the defendant is on trial is not significant."

---

[51] *Commonwealth v. Odell*, 34 Mass. App Ct. 100 (1993).

Mother's Justice

I attended religious school at the New Haven Jewish Community Center afternoons after public school. The teachers there disciplined students physically with rulers and books. I remember once complaining to my mother that I had done nothing wrong and did not deserve the punishment. She pronounced me guilty and said that maybe I would have a nicer teacher the next year. I didn't.

I now think about this scene from my childhood when I recall a very sensitive case I presided over where a male student inappropriately touched a female student at their high school. The school administration and then the police performed investigations. The boy was charged in court with indecent assault and battery and he was found guilty after a trial.

The boy's mother and the boy responded by suing the school and the assistant principal, claiming negligence and infliction of emotional distress because the mother had not been notified, pursuant to school policy, immediately after the female student first complained of the assault. Although there was an assertion that the boy did not want his mother notified, it was conceded that the school policy required such notification. Another judge and I presided over various motions and ultimately I dismissed the case.

The mother and the boy appealed to the Appeals Court and my dismissal of the lawsuit was affirmed. The Appeals Court concluded that the plaintiffs' case failed because the delay in notifying the mother could not have affected the criminal conviction because the boy had been proven guilty by an independent court of law and, furthermore, the delay could not be the legal cause of emotional distress.[52]

---

[52] *Jones v. Mahoney*, 74 Mass. App. Ct. 745 (2009). The Appeals Court noted that proof of "extreme and outrageous" conduct was necessary to prove emotional distress.

The Length and Breadth of Healthcare

This case is especially memorable to a judge with a son with special needs.

Two sibling children with special needs benefitted greatly from physical therapy throughout the year. Their mother's current health plan provided coverage for unlimited physical therapy. After a few years, the mother was informed that a new group insurance policy limited coverage for physical therapy to periods of three months per year for each illness. The health plan however, continued to provide unlimited physical therapy to the disabled children for the next three years. The mother was then informed that the limited benefits would be enforced. After three more months of therapy, further coverage was denied for the remainder of the year and the mother sued the health plan. An arbitrator ordered the health plan to continue the coverage. The arbitrator's decision was silent as to whether the health plan was to continue the full coverage for just the remainder of the year or for succeeding years too.

The health plan sought clarification from the court. The mother's attorney argued that the plan had voluntarily provided the unlimited coverage to the family for the previous three years and thus the insurer bound itself to continue the coverage.

The case was assigned to me and I offered to seek clarification from the arbitrator as to the intended duration of his ruling. The attorneys for the health plan and the mother declined my offer. After a hearing, I found there was a new agreement each year because the health plan had an annual open enrollment period when changes to the agreement were made. Even though I felt a special sympathy for the mother, the plan had never bound itself in writing to provide unlimited physical therapy coverage in perpetuity for this one subscriber only. My order essentially limited the coverage to three months.

The mother appealed my decision. The Appeals Court agreed with my ruling that each year a new contract between the health plan and its subscribers comes into existence and the plan's benevolence in providing the coverage for three years did not bind them in perpetuity.[53] I wonder if the Affordable Care Act would have influenced the outcome.

---

[53] *Harvard Community Health Plan, Inc. v. Zack*, 33 Mass. App. Ct. 649 (1992).

Oh Sleep! It Is a Gentle Thing[54]

Recently at the Boston Symphony, the man seated to my left had his eyes closed during much of Dvorak's Cello Concerto in B Minor. Occasionally, a person in a neighboring pew closes his eyes during a sermon. These events bring to mind a quote from an appellate case that "Meditation may be mistaken for somnolence."[55] Although we tend to chuckle about such things, this is a serious and recurring matter for trial judges when you consider that trials can be tedious for the jurors who are often cramped for days in overheated courtrooms. The inability to be, or appear to be, totally alert all of the time is a human condition that affects us all.

During the trial of a sexual assault case, the prosecutor came to the sidebar with defense counsel and noted that a juror in the middle of the front row had nodded off. Neither the defendant's attorney nor I had noticed it even though I always pay close attention to the jury. I then asked the court officer to keep a watchful eye on the jury and on that juror in particular. There were no concerns for the remainder of the trial. The jury found the defendant guilty.

On appeal, the defendant's appellate lawyer sought a new trial on grounds that I had not interrupted the trial and investigated the matter because the juror could have been excused if he were found to have fallen asleep. The Appeals Court ruled that I had not abused my discretion by asking the court officer to keep an eye on the juror. It noted that the prosecutor's report had not provided a basis for concluding that the nodding off was more than momentary or that it indicated inattentiveness.[56]

This was a missed opportunity for the appellate court to school trial judges on what steps to take when the inattention of a juror is observed by the judge or brought to the judge's attention. With eyes open or shut, the degree of human attention probably ebbs and flows for the judge and each juror. I wonder if a different standard should exist for criminal cases where a unanimous jury decision is required and arguably a single inattentive juror would vitiate a unanimous verdict. I can recall a couple of cases over the years where, with the agreement of the attorneys, I designated a particular juror as an

---

[54] Samuel Taylor Coleridge, "The Rime of the Ancient Mariner" (text of 1834).
[55] *Commonwealth v. Keaton*, 36 Mass. App. Ct. 81, 87 (1994).
[56] *Commonwealth v. Rafael Vasquez*, 982 N.E. 2d 73 (2011).

alternate juror because of his apparent inattention or confusion during the trial.

Attorneys have told me that they have awakened judges and jurors by intentionally dropping a book on the courtroom floor or by feigning a coughing spell. I suppose these situations confront educators on a daily basis.

Why Pick on Me?

It is easy to feel picked on; in other words, to feel singled out unfairly by someone. We might ask ourselves, "Why am I the only one on the block who didn't receive a newspaper this morning?" Or, more distressingly, "Why am I being audited by the IRS?"

The defendant inmate tried to raise a similar issue. He was in the prison yard with dozens of other prisoners when guards, who had been tipped off by another inmate, approached him and demanded that he submit to a search of his person. The defendant responded by running from them. The guards followed in hot pursuit and when they were close to a building, observed the defendant throw something onto the roof. They retrieved a knife from the roof. The defendant was not only disciplined in the prison by being placed in solitary confinement, he was also charged in court with a felony weapons violation. His case came before me. His lawyer wanted me to dismiss the case on grounds of "prosecutorial bias" or "selective prosecution." I would not dismiss the case. The jury found the defendant guilty and I imposed an additional sentence. He appealed.

The man claimed on appeal that the prison system always handled this type of matter internally with prison discipline and that they never sought additional punishment by bringing charges in court. He claimed they were unfairly biased against him because he was outspoken and was considered to be a troublesome inmate. In other words, he claimed I erred in not dismissing his case because he was placed in a position of disadvantage because he was exercising certain constitutional rights.

Given how really dangerous it must be for almost everyone in the vicinity of a prisoner who is carrying a deadly weapon, it is not surprising that the appellate court was not persuaded by his bias argument and they affirmed the conviction.[57]

---

[57] *Commonwealth v. Smith*, 40 Mass. App. Ct. 770 (1996).

Second Time Around, My First Reversal

It is fundamental constitutional law that one cannot be tried twice for the same crime. This means that once the trial formally commences, the constitutional protection of double jeopardy attaches and the case must proceed unless the defendant agrees to start again. Every first-year law student learns that jeopardy in a jury trial attaches when the jury is sworn to render a just verdict and, in a nonjury trial, when the first witness is sworn to tell the truth.

A driving under the influence (DUI) case was set for trial before another judge. He was wrapping up another case in his session and asked me if I would select a jury for him in the DUI case and he would try it as soon as he was free. The lawyers agreed and I empaneled a jury that morning and directed them to report to the other judge's courtroom at a particular time. The intended trial judge then realized that he was assigned to another courthouse the next day. Rather than trying to arrange to stay at the courthouse for the following day and without conferring with the lawyers, he declared a mistrial and scheduled the case for another day. No one objected.

I was the trial judge when the case was scheduled for a new jury trial. The defendant's lawyer had done some research and sought a dismissal on grounds of double jeopardy in that a jury had previously been sworn and jeopardy had attached. I denied the motion because the attorney had not complained when the judge excused the first jury. I empaneled a jury and the defendant was tried and convicted. He appealed and the Appeals Court reversed the conviction.[58]

The Appeals Court was kind to me and focused its criticism on the judge who could have asked to remain at the court to try the case with the empaneled jurors or at least should have met with the attorneys at the time in an effort to gain the assent of the defendant's attorney. The blame was at least partly mine. I should have remembered my first-year criminal law course.

---

[58] *Commonwealth v. Phillips*, 12 Mass. App. Ct. 486 (1981).

Lingering Thoughts on Murder

The Supreme Judicial Court recently affirmed the first-degree murder conviction in a case tried before me.[59] While reading the appellate decision, I relived the awful facts of the case that brought tears to my eyes then and now. There was a senseless killing of an unarmed boy who was a bystander. The brutal assault was fueled by alcohol, drugs, weapons, bravado, and a disregard for the sanctity of human life.

The defendant and his co-defendant, males in their twenties, were armed with knives and had consumed substantial amounts of drugs and alcohol while attending an evening city fireworks display with their girlfriends. Afterward, there was a heated confrontation between the defendant's girlfriend and an unarmed male whom the co-defendant's girlfriend punched in the face. The man pushed her down against a fence. The defendant chased him with a knife and inflicted a superficial wound to the man's back as he kept running away.

Two uninvolved teenaged boys were behind the injured man and they ran, too. The co-defendant stabbed one boy and, moments later, the defendant fatally stabbed the other boy at least seven times, perhaps with the aid of the co-defendant. The boy who died was 16 years old. His 17-year-old friend survived.

At the defendant's trial, his girlfriend testified that an unidentified person jumped on the defendant's back and was thrown off before the deceased was stabbed. No one else testified to this. Defense counsel suggested that it was the 16-year-old victim who had jumped on the defendant.

The defense at trial was that it was the co-defendant who stabbed the victim and that the defendant was merely present. I was asked to instruct the jury that, should they find that the defendant was involved, they should find him guilty of the lesser crime of manslaughter on grounds that he was acting in the heat of passion provoked by sudden combat.

I ruled that there was insufficient evidence of provocation to warrant such an instruction. I was not asked to instruct the jury on the defense of the use of excessive force in self-defense which, if successful, would have resulted in a manslaughter verdict. Upon request, such an instruction is warranted if there is any evidence, credible or not, supporting it.

---

[59] *Commonwealth v. Spinucci*, 472 Mass. 872 (2015).

The defendant was found guilty by the jury and, on appeal, the Supreme Judicial Court agreed that I was not required to instruct the jury on provocation given the state of the evidence. I was relieved that the appellate court did not rule that I was required to instruct the jury on "excessive force in self-defense," a defense that was not raised, probably for good reason because it would have been contrary to the man's primary defense that he did not participate in the stabbing. Had that been the ruling, a new trial would have been required and the victim's family would have suffered anew.

This was the last time I presided over a murder trial. In the approximately two dozen murder cases tried before me, only two persons were found "not guilty," while several were found guilty of second-degree murder, which carries a sentence of life in prison with a parole eligibility after 15 years. Perhaps two were convicted of the lesser offense of manslaughter. About twelve persons were convicted of first-degree murder and were sentenced to natural life, which is life in prison without the possibility of parole. Only one or two of these persons had put together over time a real plan to kill their victim. All of the others were involved in avoidable confrontations lasting seconds or a few minutes at most. Imagine, a brutal indiscretion lasting only moments cost each one of them the opportunity of ever living again in society.

Confounded Interest

The Massachusetts General Laws award prevailing litigants a windfall when interest is added to a court judgment. From the date of the filing of a suit to the final resolution on appeal, the prevailing party receives interest at a rate of 12% per year. The stated purpose of the law is to compensate the party for loss of use of the money. But why at 12% when the rest of society receives interest on their savings at a rate lower than 1%? For example, if a party were awarded $50,000 at trial and the case had been pending trial for three years, the pre-judgment interest would amount to 36%. If the appellate process took two more years, the post-judgment interest would be 24%. At the end of the day, the plaintiff's award would have grown from $50,000 to $80,000. The legal insiders' rationale for this windfall system is that it encourages settlements and discourages appeals. I always have "sticker shock" when I see the final computation on the amount of a judgment.

Recently, an additional windfall event in a case coupled with the interest windfall impelled me to adjust the judgment downward. The Appeals Court affirmed my ruling, but the Supreme Judicial Court reversed it.[60]

A builder had converted an old mill building to luxury condominiums. His work on the windows and roof was pretty shoddy. The plaintiffs, who were the trustees of the condominium association, did not make the necessary repairs at the time the shoddy work was discovered but instead waited almost a decade until trial to get repair and replacement estimates which, of course, would be substantially higher by then.

At trial, the plaintiffs wanted me to assess damages at the increased cost to repair ten years after the harm was discovered and then apply the 12% statutory interest of more than 60% to that sum. That was too much for me to countenance and I summarily reduced the current repair estimates by 20%, believing that inflation over ten years had increased the price of repair well over 20%. The 12% per annum interest was then applied.

---

[60] *Wyman v. Ayer Properties, LLC,* 83 Mass. App. Ct. 21 (2012), *Wyman v. Ayer Properties, LLC,* 469 Mass. 64 (2014). This case is also noteworthy because the Supreme Judicial Court, as a matter of first impression, ruled that the "economic harm" doctrine will no longer bar tort damages where there is no contract between the builder and the condominium association.

The Appeals Court found that my adjustment as to damages was reasonable under the circumstances. However, the Supreme Judicial Court disagreed and reversed both the Appeals Court and me on that facet of the case. The court did not rule that my theory was necessarily wrong, only that I had no basis in the facts to reduce it by 20%.

I can't disagree with that. I do feel that someone, someday is going to do something about the interest windfall. As a matter of fact, within recent years, the legislature amended the law to reduce the rate of interest in most medical malpractice cases.[61]

---

[61] M.G.L. Chapter 231, §60K reduced the rate of interest in suits against healthcare providers to a rate dependent on the US Treasury yield plus 2% except for wrongful death judgments, where the rate remains 12%.

True Confessions

I am grateful to the Chaffee Writers, that band of authors who meet above the food cooperative in Rutland, Vermont, each Friday from 11 AM to 1 PM. I suppose they look upon my wife Lynn and me as "summer soldiers and sunshine patriots" because we attend sessions only from mid-May through mid-October. My writing has improved immeasurably from their critiques of my previous week's writing. At a recent meeting, one of the members asked me what I did when the case before me was uneventful, uninteresting, unending, and underwhelming. I felt compelled to tell the truth, the whole truth, and nothing but the truth about what I did during rare instances of extreme boredom.

I like to think that I developed multitasking skills as a schoolboy listening to Brooklyn Dodgers baseball games while doing my homework. Many judges bring extra work to the bench during lengthy jury trials where the judge appears to be an umpire ruling on objections from the attorneys. I proofread my recent decisions and reviewed motions for the upcoming motions sessions. Concentrating on two things at the same time reminds me of Robert Frost's poem "The Investment" where the potato digger who stood in a field of unearthed potatoes was "counting out winter dinners, one a hill, with half an ear to the piano's vigor." Engaging in a second activity can help keep one alert for both.

On a lighter note, I have listened to and watched jury trial proceedings while performing isometric exercises and leg stretching routines. Occasionally, I have flipped through a few French language cards or tied a reverse bowline nautical knot or a surgeon's fishing knot without looking down. I have kept a baseball on the bench during baseball season and sometimes grasped it according to the grip depicted on my tie. I could never throw a slider, but it looked as if I could.

It is impossible to function without a lapse from time to time. Surgeons, therapists, teachers, and judges know this. Dwight Evans, the great Red Sox right fielder, says that it was relatively easy to develop the physical skill to play at challenging Fenway Park, but almost impossible to concentrate without lapses when the ball may not be hit to right field for an entire game. When I missed a question or did not understand fully the objection to a lawyer's question, I would simply look at the examining attorney and say, "Counsel, would you please rephrase your question?"

On a more serious note, I followed the practice of my mentor, the late Chief Justice William B. Bryant, who, during the presentation of gruesome evidence, found a spot on the ceiling in the rear of the courtroom and stared at it.

Judges really are, and should be, like everyone else, human.

My baseball tie

Appellate Courts

A word on appellate courts is necessary as their decisions have helped me single out those of my cases I deem to be "enduring."

As a law student in Washington, DC, I often attended "Decision Monday" at the United States Supreme Court and listened attentively to the judicial luminaries of the Warren Court read their opinions aloud. I regarded appellate courts then as near deities who dispensed true justice from on high.

In more recent years, judicial colleagues who have been appointed to appellate courts have given me an inside view of the very human appellate decision-making process. Although our appellate judges may be splendid jurists, I no longer see them as deities. I do maintain great respect for their decisions, partly because my experience with juries teaches that two or more heads are better than one. That, coupled with their superior resources of staff attorneys and law clerks as well as having the luxury of time for reflection, discussion, and writing, gives them an advantage over us trial judges, who often must share the services of a single law clerk and sometimes make snap decisions.

There is an understandable healthy tension between appellate courts and trial courts. Appellate courts correct mistakes made by trial judges. A trial judge may make tens of contested evidentiary and other rulings in the course of a trial. Mistakes are inevitable. Moreover, an appellate court may reverse a trial judge who is taking the law in a direction that the appellate court deems inappropriate. It may also reverse a trial judge's decision where the law is evolving or is in need of a change.

When I, as a trial judge, made critical and controversial decisions in a public arena under pressure with time constraints and few resources at my disposal, there was an adrenaline rush and sense of satisfaction that linger to this day.